INSIGHT INTO

PERFECTIONISM

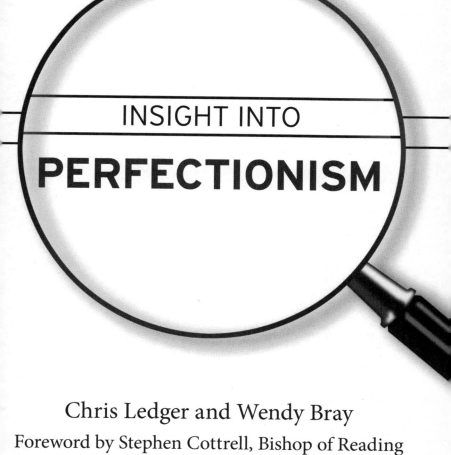

INSIGHT INTO

PERFECTIONISM

Chris Ledger and Wendy Bray

Foreword by Stephen Cottrell, Bishop of Reading

CWR

WAVERLEY ABBEY
INSIGHT SERIES

The Waverley Abbey Insight Series has been developed in response to the great need to help people understand and face some key issues that many of us struggle with today. CWR's ministry spans teaching, training and publishing, and this series draws on all of these areas of ministry.

Sourced from material first presented on Insight Days by CWR at their base, Waverley Abbey House, presenters and authors have worked in close co-operation to bring this series together, offering clear insight, teaching and help on a broad range of subjects and issues. Bringing biblical understanding and godly insight, these books are written both for those who help others and those who face these issues themselves.

CONTENTS

7

FOREWORD

G.K. Chesterton put it rather well: 'If a job's worth doing, it's worth doing badly!' By this I don't think he meant you shouldn't try to do the job well, nor that you shouldn't always give it your best shot, it's just that in all of life, and especially in the Christian life, thinking you should only do things if you can do them excellently is a recipe for disaster, and is one treacherous step away from that addiction to 'being perfect' that this book so eloquently analyses.

In this helpful and perceptive little book, and drawing on their own experience and study, Chris Ledger and Wendy Bray don't only give insights into the nature of perfectionism; they give practical pointers to help people deal with it. You see we can't all be excellent at everything. And even with the things we do well we can't be excellent all the time. If we judge our self-worth on performance and by the accolades of others then the bar will keep on being raised and sooner or later we will fall. We will become addicted to praise; obsessed by criticism. We will be less like the people God intends us to be. At worst, we become the sort of person who doesn't need God at all; after all we are striving to be perfect ourselves!

The Christian faith offers good news: I am loved and valued by God regardless of my performances or my reviews. God delights in the offerings we make because we make them honestly and humbly. God is not holding up score cards. There are no telephone votes in heaven. No eliminations. We are all included in; not because of our brilliance, but because of God's love and of what He has won for us in Jesus Christ.

Of course we try to do the best we can with the gifts we've been given, but we are set free from the nagging negativity which says that unless what we offer is the very best possible then it is not worth offering at all. Our God honours the widow's few pence just as much as the rich man's fat cheque.

Perfectionism never thinks being yourself is good enough, never thinks your offering is worthy enough. It always looks enviously on the gifts and achievements of others. The Christian way is different. God does want to change us – but not into someone else. God wants to change us into the person we are capable of becoming. And this means living with our limitations and offering all that we are to Him – warts included.

God has a picture in His heart of what we can become. His Spirit can renew and reform all those things in our life which confound and confuse this image. And when we fall, His arms are always there to hold us. So let this book help you let go of perfectionism and its false gods and take hold of grace which comes from the living God, our Saviour, Jesus Christ.

Stephen Cottrell
Bishop of Reading

INTRODUCTION

It was the actress Sadie Frost who said, 'We are all so obsessed with the perfect pout, the perfect this, the perfect that. I myself used to be a chronic perfectionist. Perfection, I've learnt, doesn't bring happiness. Perfection is a curse.'

The search for perfection never ends. Instead, it binds us into a no-win situation – often for life.

Society increasingly demands perfection. We must have the perfect home, be the perfect parent and live the perfect lifestyle.

Some of us will do things again and again in the search for perfection. We will start a letter, misspell a word halfway down the page and begin again, smudge the same word on our second attempt and reach for yet another sheet of crisp white paper, fearful of a third error. We find ourselves having to redo the simplest of tasks because what we do isn't quite perfect. Whatever we achieve or accomplish, however great the accolades, success doesn't feel quite good enough.

Others will feel under constant pressure to do everything right first time, *every* time and may even put off doing things, always procrastinating, fearing the end result won't 'make the grade'.

Because accomplishment and performance give us the feel-good factor, we reach an extreme in needing that feel-good buzz and end up wanting to do everything perfectly in order to maintain our position and retain the 'buzz'.

Our desire for perfection can dominate our lives, especially when we project our perfectionism onto other people and demand perfection from them, too. Having a perfectionist in the family might keep our kitchen worktops tidy, but long term it can cause tension between family members, and even repeated conflict.

Perfectionism may even have been bred within our family, where the mantra upholds its demands: 'Sit up straight'; 'Be a good girl'; 'You can do better than that!' Even collective wisdom and fable tell us to improve: 'If a job is worth doing … it is worth doing well'; 'If at first you don't succeed … try, try again'.

Of course, there's nothing wrong with aiming for the best. But if we have grown up experiencing too much emphasis on how our behaviour is evaluated, corrected and rewarded, we soon learn that in order to obtain approval, we must attain certain standards. The pressure to meet those standards will inevitably leave us striving to be perfect. The child becomes the adult, the adult becomes the worker and partner and so our perfectionism follows us into our adult homes, relationships, marriages and workplaces like a demanding and unwanted visitor.

But perfectionism is not all bad. If perfectionism is a burden for us we can lighten its load. We can learn to apply some balance so that we pursue the search for excellence in a healthy way.

This book aims to help us find that balance; to share understanding of perfectionism, and to introduce skills to help bring about change. It considers the way perfectionism shapes our lives and how it influences our behaviour and emotions. Most importantly, it offers insight into what God says about striving for perfection and reminds us that we are each a 'work in progress'.

Chris Ledger and Wendy Bray

Note: The reflections and activities at the end of each chapter are designed for the reader who wants to work through perfectionism in his or her own life, but they could be adapted to be used by someone accompanying another person in their journey.

CHAPTER 1

WHAT IS PERFECTIONISM?

HOW IS PERFECTIONISM DEFINED?

The Oxford English Dictionary suggests that perfectionism is 'the uncompromising pursuit of excellence',[1] while psychiatrist David Burns, in an article in *Psychology Today*, defined perfectionists as people 'whose standards are high beyond reach or reason … who strain compulsively and unremittingly toward impossible goals and who measure their own worth entirely in terms of productivity and accomplishment'.

The psychologist Don E. Hamachek describes two types of perfectionists. First, the 'Normal' or the 'Healthy Perfectionists' who derive 'a very real sense of pleasure from the labours of a painstaking effort'. By contrast, the 'Neurotic Perfectionists' exhibit perfectionist behaviour which is unhealthy. They become neurotic and 'unable to feel satisfaction because in their own eyes they never seem to do things good enough to warrant that feeling'.[2]

Wendy Roedell argues that

> In its positive form, perfectionism can provide the driving energy which leads to great achievement. The meticulous attention to detail necessary for scientific investigation, the commitment which pushes composers to keep working through until the music realises the glorious sounds playing in the imagination, and the persistence which keeps great artists at their easels until their creation matches their conception all result from perfectionism.[3]

While on holiday in New York, Wendy (Bray) visited an exhibition at the Metropolitan Museum of Art. The curators had gathered more of Turner's paintings together than had ever been seen before. Each individual painting boldly championed the skill and genius of the artist. Yet the exhibition notes described how Turner was never satisfied with what he produced, returning again and again to the same exercises in order to perfect the painting of a cloud or the turn of a tide. When gazing at his work, so breathtakingly displayed, such perfectionism was hard to understand. It had produced brilliance and wonder but had also left the artist less than happy in his search for artistic perfection. Turner was often depressed, anxious and highly demanding of self, unable to work for long periods, becoming increasingly eccentric and depressed. Yet his artistic genius – however tortured by perfectionism – leaves a beautiful legacy for us to enjoy.

Robert Slaney, an American counselling psychologist at Penn State College of Education, researched around the negative aspects of perfectionism. He developed a test which placed individuals on various scales with regard to Standards, Order, Anxiety and Procrastination. In conclusion, he remarked that 'Both adaptive and maladaptive perfectionists rate high in Standards and Order but maladaptive perfectionists also rate high in Anxiety and Procrastination'.[4]

The negative aspects of perfectionism in its pathological state often take the form of procrastination: 'I can't start my project until I know the right way to do it'; 'I daren't start to write this book because I might fail.' And self-deprecation: 'I must be stupid! How on earth can I not be able to do this?'

Procrastination and self-deprecation induced by unhealthy perfectionism can be devastating and paralysing. They may result in low self-esteem, underachievement and, in the workplace, low productivity. Workplace colleagues can feel alienated by a workmate who seems unwilling or unable to 'pull their weight' or who, while hampered by doubts, loses time on small details of a project. As the perfectionist constantly needs to check and re-check every detail, their experience of work can lead to depression, and even to a higher risk of workplace accidents.

Adderholt-Eliot describes five characteristics of perfectionist students and teachers which contribute to underachievement: procrastination, fear of failure, the all-or-nothing mindset, paralysed perfectionism and workaholism.[5] By contrast, the positive, adaptive perfectionist may work harder for longer hours but achieve higher than average results.

In personal relationships, neurotic perfectionists often make unrealistic and unhealthy demands on family and friends and may sacrifice family and social activities in their quest for their goals, whilst in the most intimate relationships unrealistic expectations can cause significant dissatisfaction for both

INSIGHT INTO PERFECTIONISM

partners. None are helped by the demands and media messages of a 'Be the Best' world.

LIFE DEMANDS PERFECTION

Increasingly, life demands perfection. Top academic students find that it's not enough to get ten A*s at GCSE and four As at A level. They now need 'Value Added' experience which proves they are the best of the very best. No wonder high-achieving students sometimes crack emotionally under the pressure to be 'perfect'. Sport also demands the perfect ten as coaches want their teams to be top of the table. Teenagers want to be first – with the latest designer label, or the lowest – in weight.

Increasingly in the competitive worlds of sport, business and entertainment, perfection is the aim. It is not enough to take part – you have to win! At what cost? Sometimes health, sometimes money: the Beijing Olympics cost the equivalent of £12 million for every gold medal awarded!

TV, film and media encourage us to have the perfect body, the perfect teeth and the perfect skin. The search for the perfect body leads to eating disorders, low self-esteem and depression, with many young girls feeling as if they can never make the grade.

Perfection is something that is constantly fed to us by a success-hungry sector of society. It is sold as a way to find control over chaos in the belief that perfection gives a sense of security. Military training and many strict educational institutions lay down very high standards and strict boundaries to shape behaviour in order to have discipline and order in these establishments. Any vulnerability to perfectionism can be intensified by such an experience, sometimes producing a demanding, perfectionist boss who might say, 'Boarding school/the army never did me any harm!' The misguided equation then sometimes becomes heavy discipline = order = perfection = sense of security.

Wendy recognised a different kind of link between perfectionism and security as she recovered from two separate cancers. Increasingly she found that she was demanding (mostly subconsciously) that life, in all kinds of detail – the state of a room, the timing of a friend's arrival, a meal in a restaurant – be perfect. This was not because she expected much of others or insisted on the best that life could offer materially; no, making sure things were 'right' or 'perfect' suggested the security of life itself. If life wasn't 'wrong' (less than perfect) it couldn't 'go wrong' (be imperfect by the cancer coming back) once again.

In a similar way, feeling or looking less than perfect can make us think we have lost control. We end up feeling unacceptable; a failure. Women, and men, often become overly house-proud, sometimes developing obsessive-compulsive disorder (OCD). Such obsessive behaviour develops from a thought pattern which says, 'I must make this house perfect, otherwise I'm a terrible mother/wife/man ...' To someone caught up in such perfectionist obsession, even a spot of dust means that the whole house will become chaotic and out of control. And when it is out of control: 'I don't feel good about myself'; 'My husband will feel I'm a rotten wife, my kids will be ashamed of me'; 'The neighbours will talk about me behind my back.' In reality, the demonstration of a bit of relaxation on the housework front often means the very opposite. Through it, we may give others permission to relax.

In the workplace, a perfectionist will perceive their lack of perfection as a disaster. It will lead to a lack of self-value because 'If my work isn't perfect that means I will not be valued – I'm a useless employee.' Or, 'I am not being valued at work because I am not doing a perfect job. Actually, I am a failure.' No consideration will be given to the idea that 'I'm in the wrong job' or 'Maybe the amount of work I am being given is humanly impossible'. A perfectionist who is capable of doing the job will see things differently, saying, 'I am no good because I'm not perfect enough, therefore I have got to work harder.'

UNDERSTANDING THE NATURE OF PERFECTIONISM

There are several ways in which the nature of perfectionism is classified and understood. Some researchers characterise perfectionism as a single concept or dimension; others suggest that perfectionism consists of several related dimensions.

Canadian psychologists Paul Hewitt and Gordon Flett[6] suggest that there are three kinds of perfectionists.

1. *Self-orientated perfectionists* are those who set standards that are unrealistically high and impossible to attain. These standards are self-imposed and perfectionists use them to evaluate their own performance. When this is linked to perceived failure and negative life events, the tendency can lead to depression.
2. *Other-orientated perfectionists* set unrealistic and high standards for other people and place importance on their being perfect, with stringent evaluation. Such perfectionists may find it difficult to delegate for fear of being let down by others and may have problems with relationships and excessive anger.
3. *Socially-prescribed perfectionists* believe that high standards are imposed upon them by others. Their perception that these high standards are impossible to meet leads to social anxiety because of a real fear of being judged and then, possibly, rejected.

Psychologist Randy Frost and his colleagues[7] suggest that perfectionism is expressed through a number of characteristics:

1. EXCESSIVE CONCERN OVER MISTAKES

An individual may believe that making mistakes is synonymous with failure. People who fear making mistakes suffer with worry about being judged by others and tend to experience social anxiety.

2. HIGH PERSONAL STANDARDS

Some perfectionists believe that they are second-rate citizens when they do not achieve their expectations and reach the high standards which they have set themselves.

3. DOUBTS AND ACTIONS

Actions which are doubted are often accompanied by an exaggerated feeling that tasks and responsibilities have not been completed correctly. There is little belief in achievements and a need to check things over and over again: a behaviour which can lead to OCD.

4. NEED FOR ORGANISATION

This presents as an overly fussy obsession with neatness and order; rigidity in approach to organisation and inflexibility about the way things are done. This type of behaviour can be destructive in a team or group, as difficulties will arise with other people who may want to do things differently. Additionally, an individual may spend so much time organising and maintaining control that other important tasks are not completed. In this situation perfectionists can be accused of not 'pulling their weight' in a team.

5. HIGH PARENTAL EXPECTATIONS

Children who grow up living with an overwhelming external pressure to perform perfectly can struggle with social anxiety and shyness.

HOW DOES PERFECTIONISM REVEAL ITSELF?

Perfectionism is multifaceted and multidimensional. It often comes in disguise, creeps up on us when we least expect it, and easily deceives. As such it can present itself to us in a myriad of ways. The clearest way to unmask perfectionism is to do so in personal terms.

Perfectionism may reveal itself to me in:

- The irrational belief that I and/or others and my environment must be perfect.
- My striving to reach the ideal and my struggle never to make a mistake on the way.
- My belief that whatever I attempt in life must be done perfectly with no mistakes, slip-ups or inconsistencies.
- An attitude that constantly looks out for imperfections, weakness and failings in myself and/or others.
- The hyper-vigilance that keeps looking for any deviation from expectations or the way things 'should be'.
- The way in which I can get lost in details and forget the purpose of the task.
- My belief that no matter what I attempt it is never good enough to meet my own or anyone else's expectations. ('If only I had done better, I would be OK.')
- My assumption that if I make a bad decision it will be disastrous.
- My rigid belief system which uses the words, 'must, ought,

should': 'I *must* please everyone all the time'; 'You *ought* to do better'; 'I *should* always be in control.'

- The way in which I feel stressed when others don't do things the 'right way' (ie to *my* standards).
- The presence of an underlying motive in the fear of failure and the fear of rejection (ie 'If I am not perfect, I will fail and/or will be rejected by others').
- My rigid expectation of self and others: one that does not allow for humanity to be weak or imperfect.
- The fact that I hate making mistakes.
- The fact that I expect a great deal from myself.
- My expectation that others will share my priorities and my frustration when these expectations are not met.
- The way I find it hard to take constructive criticism and/or praise.
- The way in which I find it hard to be a team member; I am independent and rely on myself: 'I am the only one who can do this well enough.'
- My people-pleasing habit.

High expectations and clear goals are not bad in themselves: they help us do – and be – the best we can. But when they are rigid and concrete they can cause stress and anxiety. Perfectionism can undoubtedly have a positive effect, in helping others to aim high and in paying attention to necessary detail. But if we continually strive to be perfect to such an extent that we feel a failure when we're not, we will always feel as if we fall short.

HOW DOES PERFECTIONISM DEVELOP?

In an attempt to explain what makes a perfectionist, psychologists present what they call the 'integrated view'. This suggests that both genetics and experience play a role in the development of the personality: a widely held psychological viewpoint backed up by both colloquial and scientific evidence. They conclude that although we are born with certain personality traits, our emotional and behavioural responses can be affected and orientated by our experiences of life, particularly the experience of our early years. Consequently, perfectionism may develop because of:

- A parent or carer absorbed by anxiety or worry.
- Unrealistic parental expectation.
- Lack of affirmation.
- Fear of punishment or punishment avoidance.
- Living with 'Super-parents'.

Chris, in the course of her work, meets perfectionists who struggle with anxiety problems, a deep fear of failure and an overwhelming sense of insecurity. During counselling, they will often trace those problems back to the fact that their parents were worriers, inadvertently passing on their anxiety and fear to their children. Parental messages will also betray expectations of perfectionism, even on the tail end of affirmation: 'That was great … but you could have done better'; 'You look good in that outfit … but you do need to do something about your hair'.

Family specialist Rob Parsons was once a highly driven lawyer, expecting the very best of himself and everyone around him. He now confesses, with not a little shame, that when his children were small he often transferred those expectations on to them. In his book, *The Sixty Minute Father*,[8] he writes:

I remember my daughter coming home from school. She came running in, yelling, 'Dad, I got 95% in Maths!' I had two questions for that little girl: 'What happened to the 5%?' And, 'Where were you in the class order?' I'm not proud of that memory.

Rob knew that his daughter had a whole life in front of her filled with people who would only want her when she succeeded. He says that of course he wanted to motivate her to be the best she could be; however, more importantly, she needed to know that his love for her is not based on perfection, but on the fact that he is her father. He changed.

If a child lives in a climate of 'not quite good enough', acceptance will come not from being 'themselves' but only from being someone who gets perfect grades, comes first or who always looks perfectly turned out.

One of the reasons God designed families was so that the affirmation of our parents would help us to grow up with a sense of value and worth. But of course our parents are human too, and they have their own parental messages still ringing in their ears. They will inevitably play us messages that are unhealthy, some of which their parents sent to them.

Some parents withhold affirmation believing that depriving their children of praise will make them work harder. Chris often encounters adults in a counselling situation who knew little or no praise and affirmation as children. When asked, 'How did you experience affirmation as a child?' they will reply, 'What do you mean?' They reveal that they have almost no understanding – if any – of the word 'affirmation' and no experience of being loved just for who they are. Some will grow up never hearing a simple 'Well done'. They long for that to happen, involve themselves in relationships where they think they might hear those words – but often don't. The voice of non-approval becomes internalised in the child to such an extent that they are still replaying it years later, living in drivenness and perfectionism long after both parents cease to have direct physical influence.

Mark Yaconelli[9] tells the story of a girl who grew up with alcoholic parents who were never around to attend school events. In order to cope, she threw herself into her academic work and resisted friendships, fearful of being hurt further. At her high school graduation, she walked across the stage to the sound of silence, while every other student did so with the whoops and cheers of family and friends ringing in their ears. When she graduated from college, she paid fellow students to cheer her as she walked onto the stage, but they were distracted at the crucial moment and once more the silence was deafening. Years later, newly and happily married, her husband decided to make amends and, for a surprise, played the video tape of her graduation at her birthday party. Knowing how ashamed she was of the cheer-less tape, he had added a multilayered soundtrack of himself cheering and whistling and calling her name. He thought she would at last feel loved and affirmed. But sadly, even that was too painful, and she ran from the room in tears. It took her some time to accept that she was loved so much for who she was, and to live accordingly.

The fear of punishment also feeds perfectionism. In some families, children learn that if they succeed all is well, but if they 'fall short' they will be punished. The punishment reinforces their belief that they are not good enough. If the bar they must reach is lifted ever higher by inconsistent parenting, they can go on believing that nothing will ever help them escape the pain of failure.

Then there are the Super-parents. The impact of having a very capable Superwoman or Superman as a parent can be damaging and far-reaching, because Super-parents never acknowledge their weaknesses and vulnerabilities, or the fact that they too make mistakes. They inadvertently disallow any of these very human traits in their children, whatever they might say to the contrary: 'That's beautiful, but …'; 'We don't make a mess, do we?' Children inevitably want to follow the same model as their parents and will therefore feel that they must be a Super-person too. So they become perfectionists: 'I must keep going and not give up until I am perfect.'

Our experiences of childhood or parental perfectionism often become projected onto our relationship with God. In longing to hear His 'Well done' we strive for perfection and linger too long in legalism: 'If I join this and that church committee', 'If I go to church every Sunday without fail', 'If I have every version of the Bible and know them all by heart' then I'll be good enough; I'll get my 'Well done' from God. None of those activities are wrong in themselves. But they might display an unhealthy striving based on performance and 'doing the right thing', not to mention taking us away from family, friends and a healthy lifestyle.

What we often forget is that God wants us to put our relationship with Him before rules. His love for us is unconditional. Unconditional love says, in words and actions: 'I approve of you, of who you are, regardless of what you have done.' The place of longing to be accepted and loved, to please and delight, is a healthy, God-given place to be. But we need to know how to maintain a healthy balance in that longing, so that we perform to the best of our ability, rather than strive to perform to perfection.

WHAT DOES GOD MEAN BY 'BEST' AND 'PERFECT'?

God wants us to aim for His goals and to live by His standards. He does not intend us to live in a way in which we put undue pressure on ourselves to achieve or always feel that we are not good enough.

God longs for us to live life to the full (John 10:10). He wants the best for us. But that best is His best, not ours. We need to understand that His best does not mean 'perfect'. Once we've grasped that fact we can find a healthier way to live life to the full, as He intends.

As Christians, we are called to be holy (Lev. 19:2). Holy means being 'called to be set apart from the world as God's own people'.[10] And perhaps that's where the problems start: we confuse the word 'holy' with the word 'perfect'. In effect, we take the wholeness out of holiness. God doesn't expect us to be perfect – He knows us too well!

We can spend so much time trying to be perfect that we miss out on God's acceptance and encouragement, the very things that offer us wholeness as part of our holiness. We rightly set goals for our personal and spiritual development, but instead of helping us to grow into the wholeness – and holiness – we seek, those goals often make us emotionally neurotic. We become bound by our harsh self-expectations and self-criticism when we don't reach the targets we have set ourselves.

We need to understand what God says – and really means – about perfection. Yet even when we turn to the Bible for guidance, our interpretation of what we read is sometimes mistaken and not at all helpful. Undoubtedly, the first verse that pops into our minds is: 'Be perfect, therefore, as your heavenly Father is perfect' (Matt. 5:48). But Jesus is setting a goal or a standard for perfect love here, not insisting on perfect behaviour. The Hebrew understanding of 'perfect' means moving towards fulfilment. An accomplished artist knows that his or her work will not be perfect from the first brushstroke. Often it looks a mess before it looks marvellous! But the artist has high standards: perfection is the goal. Anything less would result in a less than perfect painting. So, stroke by stroke, moment by moment, the work becomes more and more the thing it was designed to be. The closer it comes to completion, the more perfection can be seen in it: a glimmer here, a suggestion there. It is going on towards being perfect, but perfection will only be seen when it is brought to an end by completion. That's how God sees us: as a work in progress, going on towards completion when at last perfection will be seen. For now, He sets standards and goals of love and behaviour to help us on our way. But they are hopes/desires – *goals* – not expectations, because He knows that anything less than high standards will not encourage us to reach our best.

So, every one of us is a work in progress. God isn't finished with us yet! We will not be perfect until we are with God Himself, but we are to go on edging closer, learning, listening, and maturing until we meet Him face to face; always growing closer, always growing more and more like Jesus – who *is* perfect.

Wendy's daughter has a penchant for clothes. She would love to be able to purchase a designer dress or two, but instead must make do with the off-the-peg high street versions of the heavenly, perfect outfits she so craves. 'One day …' she says, sighing at the Alice Temperley dresses in Selfridges that are so out of her reach. Meanwhile, she emulates that 'heavenly perfection' in every way she can. While copying the designer's style within a more down-to-earth price range and saving hard, she lives with the hope that one day she will own the 'real thing'.

In a sense, we are moving towards our own heavenly perfection outfit: one that will suit us for eternity. For now it's out of reach, and we say 'One day ...' But we can still work towards it.

If we are perfectionists, we often face a demand to be all or nothing. In our eyes we feel we must either be perfect or not perfect. So the perfectionists among us especially need to understand that we are all growing into that place of wholeness and perfection as we 'go on and grow on' into maturity. How do we do that?

God asks us to 'go on growing on' by:

- Growing in character – longing to be more like Jesus.
- Growing in spiritual maturity – in understanding, faith and discipline.
- Growing in love – a genuine desire to love others as God loves us.
- Growing in holiness – seeing ourselves as set apart to live God's way.

In the final chapter, we will look more closely at the practicalities of nurturing such spiritual growth.

Growing towards perfection means becoming mature enough to give ourselves to others as we give ourselves to God. Jesus illustrated this kind of giving during His conversation with a rich young man, when He said, 'If you want to be perfect, go, sell your possessions and give to the poor, and you will have treasure in heaven. Then come, follow me' (Matt. 19:21). Here, Jesus explained how to be whole, complete – *perfect* – in God's sight: by giving. 'We can be perfect if our behaviour is appropriate for our maturity level – perfect, yet with much room to grow.'[11] Growth through giving is our goal.

The apostle Paul knew that he was a work in progress when he said, 'Not that I ... have already been made perfect, but I press on to take hold of that for which Christ Jesus took hold of me' (Phil. 3:12). This goal absorbed all of Paul's energy. He recognised that he would never be able to perfectly express Christ to others, but he committed himself to God's work, pressing on towards his goal.

Paul was also convinced that a new freedom came in Christ: a freedom which largely transformed many of the assumptions of the old Law. In the book of Hebrews, we read that 'The former regulation is set aside because it was weak and useless' (7:18), that the Law appointed 'as high priests men who are weak' – the reason why Jesus came as a priest – and that 'the Son ... has been made perfect for ever' (7:28) – Jesus is the one and only truly perfect Person.

The Law was never intended to save people and make them perfect but to show us our need of salvation and the freedom it would give. Rules and regulations are no help if we want to draw near to God in true and honest relationship. However, Jesus does draw us close to Himself and to His Father. He bids us come 'just as we are' so that we can stand before Him accepted, loved and valued. What counts is not *our* perfect work but *God's* perfect work – work done on the cross through Jesus. Despite living a perfect life, Jesus took all our wrongdoing (sin) upon Himself so that we could be reconciled with God the Father. He continues this work today through the Holy Spirit, as He turns His heart towards us in undeserved love and forgiveness. It is only in this context – as we become more like Him – that we can be made perfect.

Instead of striving and struggling, we can simply allow ourselves to be accepted by Him, be committed to follow Him and to live in His grace (undeserved favour): grace that says, 'Yes, your best is good enough. It is my desire simply for you to go on growing in faith and love, and I know that right now you are doing your best.' Faith and love are, in a sense, the goals of our life's journey.

A life journey taken without God is often rooted in the bondage of control. It says, 'Do this and *that* will happen. If you do everything perfectly, you will get everything you want and deserve.' Such an expectation may possibly lead to fulfilment – but it may equally lead to emptiness and dissatisfaction and leave us far from reaching our goals.

A life journey taken with God is rooted in the freedom of grace – God's unmerited, unearned favour towards us. It says, 'Go out into life, love and give and do your best. Not because doing things God's way will mean an easy, prosperous life, but because God will be glorified in that life.' That expectation leads to God and to the words 'Well done, good and faithful servant' (Matt. 25:21).

Therefore we have a choice – to live striving for our own perfection, or to live freely in God's acceptance, grace and mercy as a much-loved work in progress. Which will we choose?

By making the choice to live God's way, in grace and freedom, many of us will recognise that perfectionism has become a habit that we now know we need to break. Freedom from the pressure of perfectionism is a liberation some of us long for. We know we can claim all God has for us and be released from perfectionism. But to be free for good, we must both understand how perfectionism became habitual in the first place and understand what it is that has kept us imprisoned in that habit for so long.

ACTIVITY

On a large piece of paper, write down some of the ways in which you think you should be perfect, eg

'I believe I must always be immaculately suited and booted.'
'I must always leave my desk cleared when I leave the office at 5.30.'
'I should always iron my tea towels.'
'I'm the boss so I mustn't be seen to make any mistakes.'

REFLECTION

- Now read the section entitled 'What does God mean by "best" and "perfect"?' (p.26) again. What does this say to you?
- Take a few quiet moments to reflect on your thoughts.
- Perhaps you are reading this book because someone close to you struggles with perfectionism, and you want to help them. Think of them now.

PRAYER

Lord God, as I begin this journey to understand perfectionism, please travel beside me. Let me know that You are with me every step of the way. Help me discern truth from falsehood, reality from fantasy, the impossible goal from the possible dream. Help me understand that in Your eyes I am a perfect work in progress, in Christ Jesus Your Son. Amen.

NOTES

1. Oxford Compact English Dictionary (Oxford: Oxford University Press, 1996).

2. W.D. Parker and K.K. Atkins, 'Perfectionism and the Gifted', *Roeper Review*, 17 (3), 1994, pp.173-176.

3. Wendy C. Roedell, 'Vulnerabilities of Highly Gifted Children', *Roeper Review*, 6 (3), 1984, pp.127-130.

4. Robert Slaney, 'The Almost Perfect Definition', (http://www.rps.psu.edu/sep96/almost.html), 1996.

5. M. Adderholt-Eliot, 'Perfectionism and Underachievement', *Gifted Child Today*, 12 (1), 1989, pp.19-21.

6. P.L. Hewitt and G.L. Flett, 'Perfectionism in the Self and Social Contexts', *Journal of Personality and Social Psychology* (hewittlab.psych.ubc.ca, 60, No.3, 1991) pp.456-470.

7. In Martin M. Antony and Richard P. Swinson, *When Perfect Isn't Good Enough* (CA: New Harbinger Publications, 1998), p.10.

8. Rob Parsons, *The Sixty Minute Father* (London: Hodder & Stoughton, 1995), pp.62-63.

9. Mark Yaconelli, from a talk given at the Greenbelt festival, 2007.

10. *The Thematic Bible* (London: Hodder & Stoughton, 1996), p.1,839.

11. *NLT Life Application Study Bible* (Wheaton, Illinois: Tyndale House, 2004).

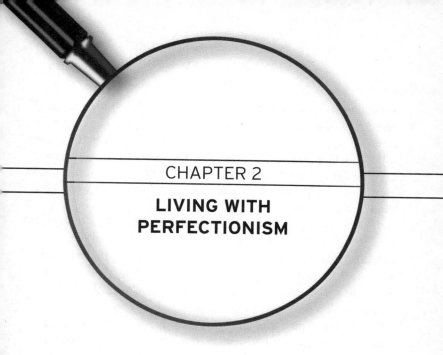

CHAPTER 2

LIVING WITH PERFECTIONISM

THE HAMSTER WHEEL

Perfectionism is usually a cycle: a veritable hamster wheel of perfectionist habits from which it is hard to escape.

First, an unrealistic goal is set which raises expectations. Then, as soon as that goal is in place, we (if we are perfectionists) begin to fear either not meeting it at all or failing to meet it as and when we expected. We can start to live under a constant pressure to achieve, padding away constantly on the wheel in order to 'get it right', and to 'get it right' always. We will find we are forever spinning harder and faster in our endless round of unrealistic goals and expectations, growing dizzy in the face of what we see as failure, even when we know success, because perfection sometimes reduces its own effectiveness. Far from recognising an achievement for what it is, we simply raise the bar of self-expectation. We can then become self-critical, self-blaming and blind to our own achievements, however excellent: 'I could have done better'; 'I am a failure'; 'I'm nobody.' Loss of self-esteem follows, which may lead to anxiety and depression. Sometimes another goal is set as the first is abandoned, then another and another in the belief that 'if only I try harder, work harder, give more, I will succeed'.

In the film *Chariots of Fire*, there is a marked difference between athlete Harold Abrahams and his fellow Olympians, Eric Liddell, Aubrey Montague and Lord Lindsay. While they train with healthy self-expectation and rejoice modestly at success, Abrahams is never satisfied, pushing himself relentlessly. Even when he achieves his Olympic silver medal he faces a crushing sense of anti-climax and a longing to hide, shrinking back from the victorious crowd of athletes as they arrive back in England.

In an earlier scene, Sybil – Abrahams' future wife – scolds him for his inability to recognise his achievements in a race where he came second. He declares that if he can't win he won't race. Sybil snaps back that if he doesn't race he won't win. But Abrahams is crushed, haunted by memories of being second at the tape.

Abrahams gave all he had to give and won his medal, but for him it was never enough; his perfectionism almost crippled him, threatening to deprive him of the ultimate prize, an Olympic medal.

To persevere may seem admirable, but perfectionists persevere without taking adequate stock of their situation and their resources. They resemble a big spender on small funds, aiming for what their money can never buy. However they rearrange their funds they'll never make that biggest of all gold-plated purchases.

So, what difference does such a driven internal motivation to achieve make?

There are six functional areas of our lives to consider:

- Physicality (physical responses and symptoms)
- Thoughts
- Beliefs
- Behaviour
- Emotions
- Spirituality

PERFECTIONISM AND PHYSICAL RESPONSES (OR PHYSICAL SYMPTOMS)

Our bodies react with physical sensations when we demand perfection from ourselves and others, to such an extent that our emotions are also continuously aroused. Some of us will recognise and respond to perfectionism by interpreting the tension it causes in our bodies, recognising that tension is an indicator of perfectionist behaviour – even learning to challenge and manage the behaviour as a result.

We may experience:

- Muscular tension
- Aches and pains
- Loss of appetite
- Comfort eating
- Headaches
- Palpitations
- Panic attacks
- An urge to run away

- Extreme tiredness
- Low immune system resulting in more coughs, colds and flu bugs

If we are perfectionists, we may be so driven by our own internal demands that we feel like a spring being squeezed into a box with a tight-fitting lid, or a pressure cooker that is about to burst its safety valve. In other words, we feel *stressed*.

Ian was a very capable forty-two-year-old high-flyer in the City of London. A perfectionist by nature, he worked all hours of the day. Even then he didn't feel he had done a good enough job. The effects of this continual internal pressure caused anxiety, trembling, palpitations, aches and pains, negative self-critical thoughts and high blood pressure. This internal stress, year in year out, eventually caused a complete breakdown in his health with subsequent burnout and he was off work for six months.

The opposite route to perfectionist behaviour can be evident when people feel so stressed that they try to take control of life by trying to make everything perfect.

Anna was a conscientious worker who enjoyed a tidy desk at work and a well-run, tidy home. But when she became very tired and frustrated with the ordinary demands of life, she found her conscientiousness tipping over into perfectionist behaviour. Because of extreme tiredness, she experienced a loss of balance in her life and began to feel very insecure. This caused Anna to overcompensate by obsessively prioritising an ultra-tidy work desk and a spick-and-span house with nothing out of place. Her fastidious perfectionism drove her work colleagues and family round the bend when she was tired!

Each area of our lives will be affected by how we choose to work out our internal motivation to achieve.

PERFECTIONISM AND OUR THOUGHTS

Our perfectionist thoughts may be kept to ourselves – but the perfectionism they demand may become all too evident.

> Jenny's friend Anne has said that she will pick Jenny up between 7.45 and 8am for a day out. When Anne hasn't arrived by 8am, Jenny is getting slightly hot under the collar. By 8.05 she is peering anxiously up and down the road, wringing her hands. Her worrying self-talk begins its frantic conversation:
>
> 'Where is she?'
>
> 'She should be here by now.'
>
> 'This is dreadful!'
>
> 'Why do people always let me down?' (Despite the fact that Anne is normally reliable.)
>
> As Jenny waits she becomes stressed, angry and exhausted, her thoughts and emotions mixing into a powerful cocktail – enough to make her lose her mind.
>
> When Anne arrives a few moments later, at 8.07, she isn't even aware that she is late. But as she turns on to Jenny's drive, she spots her friend almost leaping up and down on the doorstep. It's obvious that Jenny is furious!

Jenny is a perfectionist. As far as she is concerned, everyone else should be perfect. She is a 'socially and others-related perfectionist' – if someone says they will do something, then they should do it. If she had been aware of her own self-talk and just how irrational she was being, she might have ended up feeling, at worst, embarrassed by her anxiety and at best, oblivious to the time. She might have thought a thousand other things as she waited:

'Is my clock fast?'
'Oh good. I can put the rubbish out while I'm waiting.'
'I hope Anne hasn't broken down. It looks like rain.'
'It's not the end of the world. If there's car trouble, I can always get a taxi and pick Anne up on the way.'
'I'll wait five more minutes and then give her a call to check she's OK.'

But of course Jenny the perfectionist doesn't think that way – things have to be right, and the perfectionist self-talk tells her that this isn't right at all. The result is that Jenny and Anne start their journey with the thick cloud of Jenny's annoyance hovering between them. Anne won't apologise; she feels she has nothing to apologise for and that Jenny really must get over this. And Jenny? Well! How dare Anne be so late?

Jenny is demonstrating *All-or-Nothing Thinking*, or *Black and White Thinking*, which sets excessively high standards and is blind to the reality or practicalities of a situation. The all-or-nothing thinker will have a tendency to see things either as right or wrong, without realising that there may be a perfectly reasonable in-between. Or, like Jenny, they will assume that someone is wrong rather than the victim of circumstances. The perfectionist will hold standards for themselves and others that are unrealistic and which don't take into account what are perfectly understandable everyday situations. Out of their lips will slip the likes of:

'My reports are never good enough.'
'I seem to be the only person who washes up the office coffee mugs!'
'Why has he washed the car that way instead of my way?'
'If I eat one biscuit my diet will be ruined for life.'
'Don't they *know* which way the saucepan handles face?'

Alternatively, a perfectionist may compile a 'To Do' list for the day that is so long that it would take at least a month to work through. It is simply unrealistic. Much better, perhaps, to produce a 'To Do' list like that of Toad in the children's book *Frog and Toad Together*.[1] Toad plans the next day with a list and begins it with 'Wake up' so that he can cross something off straight away – instant sense of achievement.

Often perfectionists' self-talk extends to what they think someone else is thinking or saying. Suddenly they become expert mind-readers or develop an ability to hear an imagined conversation taking place several miles away behind locked doors! But, of course, none of us can really know what someone else is thinking or may be saying when we aren't there; in fact, some of us might even read something significant into what somebody *doesn't* say when we're with them.

When George's boss doesn't give him much feedback from a task, George assumes that this is because his boss thought his work wasn't good enough: 'My boss thinks I'm useless. It all went wrong. What did I do?' And then, 'This is awful. He'll fire me if I don't improve.' Yet George's boss has simply had a busy day and his intention to praise George fully for his brilliant efforts has slipped down his list of priorities.

Wendy's children have nicknamed her the 'bungee jumping conclusionist'! Too often, her sensitivity means that she assumes that someone hasn't done a certain thing, or thinks this, that or the other about her because of something she said or did. Thankfully she is aware of her weakness and tries to keep it in check. But many of us jump to conclusions, assuming we know what another person is thinking, based on our own expectations – even our own behaviour. That often involves imagining ourselves being judged negatively by others.

Catastrophic Thinking also grows out of perfectionist thought patterns. We blow the tiniest events out of all proportion. There's fluff on the lounge carpet and a coat on the floor in the hall – both easily dealt with. Yet our reaction is: 'This is terrible, the whole house is a complete mess!' The whole house? Every room?

Sometimes as perfectionists we will *globalise* our mistakes. Perhaps we'll make a slip-up in a presentation – hesitate because we lost our place in our notes, or pronounce a name wrong and correct it. Nobody notices the first and everybody (except us) has forgotten the second by the end of our slot. But we think, 'I made an absolute mess of it.' Yet we lost our way just once, and who wouldn't pronounce Gerdozolosiviaski wrong at first attempt! If I'm a perfectionist, however, I will think such mistakes are the worst thing in the world. I globalise my mistake.

Rigid Thinking springs from guilt and self-expectation. 'Should' and 'ought' statements abound in our thinking and self-talk ('I *should* do this'; 'I *ought* to do that'; I *must* do the other'), but the rules of how things should, ought and even must be are usually subjective, dictated by our own high standards formed into rules. If perfectionists break their own rule, the corresponding failure gives rise to feelings of guilt, inadequacy and anxiety. 'Should', 'ought' and 'must' cause significant emotional arousal because of the often unrealistic demands they make, either in ourselves or, when projecting those demands onto others, in 'other-orientated perfectionism' ('He shouldn't have done that'; 'They ought to do this'; 'She mustn't do the other'). 'Should', 'ought' and 'must' are also devoid of any willing desire regarding giving and doing. Instead, they often hide demands and unrealistic expectations behind a veil of duty and obligation.

Rigid thinking is also exposed when we believe that we are the only one who can do this or that job, or that so-and-so can't be trusted with that task, betraying our perfectionism. And, quite frankly, not a small degree of arrogance!

PERFECTIONISM AND OUR BELIEFS

When events occur in our lives, we interpret their meaning through our beliefs. Everything we see, feel and understand is experienced through belief 'spectacles'. These are fitted with a lens which evaluates our life accordingly, affirming or triggering happy or traumatic thoughts, emotions and even behaviour as a result.

Dr Judith Beck, Director of the Beck Institute for Cognitive Therapy and Research,[2] called our inner ideas about ourselves, core beliefs: 'one's most central ideas about the self'. These core beliefs 'speak' to us.

Example:

Barry is a perfectionist: he must meet every deadline at work with a perfect piece of work for him to believe he is doing a good job. One day he had a blazing row with his wife before work, and his subsequent thoughts throughout the day were so overwhelming in self-deprecation and self-hate that he forgot to save his day's work on the computer and lost it.

Situation/event
Unable to meet important deadline
↓
Hidden and unconscious core belief activated
Core belief says: 'I'm worthless.'
↓
This gave rise to automatic thoughts
'I am no good in my job because I've failed.'
↓
Distorted interpretation
'I will probably lose my job.'
↓
Reactions
Emotions aroused
Worries, anxieties, fears, guilt.

Physical sensations
Palpitations, nausea, headache.

Choice of behaviour
Barry chooses to go off sick the next day in fear of what his boss may say.

Spiritual life
'I'm a terrible Christian because I have not done a good job and have let God down.'

For the perfectionist, core beliefs say 'I'm worthless'; 'I'm terrible'; 'I'm inadequate'; 'I'll never match up'; 'I'm unlovable.'

Chris knows her core thought is 'I am inadequate'. 'I had a twin sister who was always the centre of attention and would always "get there first" in any situation where treats, rewards or special events were concerned. So my core belief was always that I was never quite quick enough, always a bit inadequate. Even now, I sometimes have to watch that I don't spiral down into that belief.'

In any event or situation Chris's hidden and unconscious belief about herself – her core belief – will give rise to automatic thoughts and self-talk, which prompts self-doubt and convinces her that whatever the situation suggests, it must be something to do with her inadequacy. How much that is the case and how much her behaviour is affected will depend on how vulnerable she is feeling at the time. She says she doesn't believe this core belief as much as she did, but still battles with it at times.

Similarly, Wendy's core belief is 'I'm a dear little thing' who will never really amount to very much. A premature baby, often ill as a child, she was overprotected and controlled by a mother who loved her very much but whose love inadvertently drained rather than encouraged her confidence and self-belief. It is something she still struggles with.

God sees our hearts and He sees us doing our best. We are worth so much more in His sight than we can comprehend, and it is His estimation of us that matters. Examining our automatic thoughts helps us to be clear about the false assumptions – or core beliefs – we carry about ourselves: assumptions that God does not share. It's sometimes easy to examine our thoughts and highlight the assumptions they contain so that both can be challenged, for example:

Thought: 'I must get it right and be perfect or something bad will happen and I will be a failure.'
Assumption: 'If I don't do it perfectly then I will be rejected.'
Thought: 'I must be perfect or someone will be angry with me.'
Assumption: 'If I don't get it perfectly right then people will get angry with me because I've failed.'
Thought: 'I must be perfect for others to accept me and give me a sense of worth in being a good Christian.'
Assumption: 'If I don't get it perfectly right then others will not accept and value me, and I believe my witness has let God down.'

But of course there is even a dilemma about what constitutes 'perfect'. Perfection, like beauty, is in the eye of the beholder. What is perfection to one person is not always perfection to another.

In the Old Testament, Samuel is searching for a new king and has in his own mind the kind of man who would be perfect, doubtless someone strong and rugged. But God says to Samuel, 'The LORD does not look at the things man looks at. Man looks at the outward appearance, but the LORD looks at the heart' (1 Sam. 16:7). God looks at our heart. He sees our motivation, not the outward appearance or performance. We are so used to people expecting our outward appearance or performance to 'measure up' that we become too dependent on their assessment of us. But God is the one we are aiming to please. It doesn't matter who else looks on or what they think. Their view is secondary. God sees the best we have been able to do, and rejoices in it.

We might say, 'If I do it perfectly, then I can relax'; 'If I do it perfectly, then I will be accepted'; 'If I do it perfectly, I can get promotion.' But God loves and accepts us *now*, whenever, wherever and whatever. There is nothing we can do to make God love us less and nothing we can do to make Him love us more.

Instead of being driven by an internal reward, God's desire is that we are driven by an *eternal* reward. The eternal reward that God gives is one that rewards faith, not perfection, with the longed-for words: 'Well done, good and faithful servant' (Matt. 25:21).

PERFECTIONISM AND OUR BEHAVIOUR

All behaviour moves towards a goal, and God gives us free will to choose how we behave. Anorexics behave in the way they do because they want to have a perfect body or are frightened of putting on weight. They want to feel in control of food, in order to achieve that goal, even if it stems from their low sense of self-worth. Similarly, it helps our understanding of perfectionist behaviour to look at the goal that is hidden beneath that behaviour.

> Sally has great difficulty choosing what clothes to buy. She fears that once she is home she will regret her choice of one outfit rather than another. So she buys several outfits to make sure she has the right one to look good in. Unfortunately she does this with everything she buys and her house is full of unwanted goods. Her core belief tells her 'I'm unlovable'. Consequently, it is important to Sally not to make mistakes. Her husband becomes angry with her because she spends too much money on her credit card and gives too much time and attention to her clothes. Wanting to be perfect leaves her home life far from perfect, but she is unable to break the cycle.

45

Of course, it's not only us and our families that are impacted by our perfectionist behaviour.

> Gary is very critical, especially with his friends. He corrects what they say and criticises what they do. His friends interpret this behaviour as his putting them down to show how smart he is: behaviour typical of someone with low self-esteem. However, in Gary's case his hypercriticism comes from an internal pressure to make things right because Gary feels an intense discomfort when things are wrong. So when mistakes are made at work, he demands that everyone gets things right and constantly lives with very unreasonable, unrealistic and often unattainable goals – as well as frustrated workmates.

Gary is driven to achieve perfection by his own inability to live without it.

The relationship between thoughts and behaviour may also work the other way around, so that behaviour affects thoughts. Behaviours often maintain beliefs because the validity of the truth has never been tested. For example, people who believe that constant checking of their work will prevent them from making a mistake are likely to continue to do so obsessively, rather than face the fact that although it would be uncomfortable to find a mistake, it would not be the end of the world. Instead, checking and rechecking maintains their anxiety and, in turn, maintains their perfectionist behaviour. Because perpetual checkers have never tested themselves in any other way, they don't know or live with the truth. They cannot approach the task in a healthy way – perhaps limiting themselves to working through the task and thoroughly checking it once – because it feels too difficult or unsafe.

It often helps those caught in the cycle of perfectionist

behaviour to be part of their own exposure experiment, in which they experience a new way of behaving in order to recognise that their feared failure is not as bad as they imagined. A woman whose obsessive housework reflects her belief that she will be seen as a dreadful person if her house is left unvacuumed for a day will maintain her thinking and behaviour by never leaving her carpets alone for more than twenty-four hours; if she has never tried living without her daily duty with a vacuum cleaner she will never learn to live in a place where she can think, 'I can live without the carpet being vacuumed every day. It doesn't make much difference to the tidiness of the house. It's not the end of the world. I can learn to be more flexible. It may even give me more time to get to know the people whose opinions and judgment I (probably needlessly) fear.'

Perfectionists who discover that their worst fear is *not* their worst fear can be truly liberated people.

So, perfectionism is illustrated by behaviours which involve:

OVERCOMPENSATING

Because perfectionism is often associated with the fear of not meeting a particular standard or performance, perfectionists sometimes work so hard in order to get things right that they overcompensate in their behaviour, working long hours or producing two alternative reports instead of one.

Maddie believes that to be promoted she must do a perfect job. Therefore she is to be found in the office at all times of the day … and night. She is overcompensating because she fears that she is not good enough. Maddie's boss may recognise her efforts as commitment, but he is just as likely to deny her promotion because her unhealthy and

47

stressful work-life balance may cause performance problems long-term. Unless he explains this to Maddie, she will think she has been passed over for promotion because she isn't good enough and work even harder – with devastating results.

EXCESSIVE CHECKING

Review and checking is a healthy occupation, but continual checking of a task betrays perfectionism. For some people this becomes OCD. Whilst obsessive checking can come about as a result of previous experience (checking that doors are locked after suffering a burglary for instance) the thought/behaviour link can cause a more serious problem.

> Caroline fears that she is not doing a good job at work in spite of knowing that she rarely makes a mistake. Her internal core belief is 'I am inadequate'. Her thoughts are: 'I shouldn't have this job'; 'A mistake will be disastrous.' Her assumption is: 'If I make a mistake then someone will find out that I'm a total failure.' Her view of her own worth and ability is distorted. So she frequently asks her supervisor to check her work, looking for constant reassurance. Her supervisor is puzzled as she trusts Caroline to do a good job and knows she always will, but is becoming increasingly irritated with Caroline's needy attitude. Rather than strengthening her internal belief that she is doing well, Caroline continually relies on someone else for a 'check up'.

PROCRASTINATION

Perfectionism may also cause procrastination: putting off tasks until later. As thoughts affect behaviour, employees who believe that a task must be completed perfectly will be more inclined to procrastinate when they fear failure, sincerely believing that whatever they produce will not be good enough so they are bound to fail. Alternatively, they know they can't possibly meet the demands they have set themselves, so would rather delay trying.

Putting off doing things for fear of never meeting internalised goals and standards can be crippling. While it's important that we have goals and standards for any task – even if they remain unspoken – it is equally important that those goals and standards are realistic and achievable and that we understand that it's OK not to meet them, for whatever reason.

Perfectionists may often avoid a situation for fear of failure or because (like Caroline) they feel they don't measure up and don't want to be exposed.

Harry has been asked for the first time to preach at a church service. He becomes so frightened that he is not going to do a perfect job that he can't get started. He knows what he wants to say, but he can't begin to put his notes together. In the end, he leaves his preparation – or rather his non-preparation – so late that he has to back out of preaching altogether. His church leader is puzzled because Harry is usually so well organised and potentially a gifted communicator.

DIFFICULTY MAKING DECISIONS
Faced with many alternatives, the perfectionists among us are often anxious about making decisions we may regret. Instead of weighing up pros and cons in a reasonable time, we doubt our own judgment and would be among the worst contestants on TV's *Who Wants to be a Millionaire?*, needing to 'phone a friend' for the answer to the first question! Our inability to decide may

also lead us to make bad choices through anxiety or because we plump for any old thing at the last moment.

> When The Cheerful Ramblers group meet for a pub lunch after their Dartmoor walk, there are always two members who keep the hungry group waiting. Sheila takes ages to decide what to order, but when she has finally done so, hears what someone else has ordered and changes her mind: this can happen several times! Bob, however, would rather others made the decision for him; then he can't blame himself when he chooses something less than delicious.

FAILURE TO DELEGATE
Because perfectionists find it difficult to trust others to get things done 'properly', ie because of the way they think those things 'should' be done, they can find it impossible to delegate.

> Alistair has been promoted and, for the first time, has his own PA. She is very experienced and competent. But instead of welcoming her appointment as an opportunity to focus on areas of his job that only he can do, he has trouble trusting her to carry out tasks, just in case she doesn't do them as he would. He spends so much time organising her work that she ends up frustrated. His bosses wonder if he was the right man for the job after all, as his time and management skills seem to have nosedived.

OVER-CRITICISM
If perfectionists are overly concerned about how things are done, they may frequently over-criticise or try to change the behaviours of others. They will not feel able to stand back and let others do things their way – even if that way turns out to be the best way.

Parents who over-criticise their children, or show them how to do everything, can raise young adults who are frustrated, over-dependent on others or lacking in confidence.

Jilly did almost everything for her two children throughout their childhood and teenage years, as she believed she knew best and wanted things to be right. Both children dropped out of higher education, ended up in a series of jobs far below their giftings and capabilities and became largely dependent on Jilly and her husband financially. When Jilly's daughter married and became pregnant, it was Jilly who went to antenatal classes with her daughter rather than her son-in-law. Jilly still had to ensure that everything was 'right'. She even told her daughter what name to give her newly born child.

PERFECTIONISM AND OUR EMOTIONS

Perfectionists will often struggle with their emotions because a sense of inadequacy leaves them feeling lacking in worth, depressed or anxious about reaching – or failing to reach – a goal. Emotional responses sometimes become physical responses manifested in panic attacks and palpitations. Anxiety reaches sky-high levels. Anger may result from blocked goals, and depression stems from guilt at not achieving what 'I ought to achieve'.

DEPRESSION

Most of us can deal with the occasional disappointment or failure. We put it down to experience and look ahead to another day. But perfectionists whose self-worth is built on the pursuit of the perfect result may find themselves in a downward psychological spiral. Depression can result from internalised suppressed anger and frustration or guilt, which accuses self of not achieving what it 'should' achieve.

> Mary began her first graduate appointment full of hope. She had
> done well at university, but found the world of work very different.
> She was working alongside high-flyers and those who had been doing
> the job for several years and, whilst they were encouraging and aware
> of her novice status, Mary struggled. She felt that she would never
> match up to what she saw as 'their' exacting standards. Instead of
> sharing her feelings with her mentor, Mary kept her frustrations
> inside and, angry at herself, quickly became depressed. It was only
> when a senior colleague recognised her younger self in Mary that
> Mary's difficulties could be addressed.

ANXIETY AND FEAR

When perfectionism becomes pronounced and unhealthy it can
produce extreme anxiety and real fear in those who are striving
for perfection. Anxiety can produce physical symptoms from
sleeplessness to panic attacks, and fear of failure can hang heavy
like a dark cloud. Perfectionists who experience anxiety and fear
can quickly imagine a worst case scenario which they sincerely
believe will befall them if they do not perform perfectly. They
jump to conclusions in their anxious state and end up under-
performing because their fear paralyses them.

> Adrian was given the opportunity of representing his company at a
> nationwide conference. As he finished his excellent presentation, he
> spotted the senior director of his company leaving the hall. Adrian
> was gripped with fear and panic: Why had he come? Was he checking
> up on Adrian? After the session, Adrian left promptly and remained
> in his hotel room, convinced that he would soon be called by his

immediate boss and asked for his resignation. When the call came, his boss congratulated him on an excellent job. Adrian learned that senior management had been considering him for promotion and that the director had called in to the conference en route to another meeting in order to catch a glimpse of Adrian in action. What he had seen had impressed. He had been disappointed not to be able to tell Adrian personally but had pressing business – hence his early departure.

INTENSE ANGER

The constant drivenness to achieve perfection can cause a build–up of suppressed anger as each failure to reach a goal occurs. It is buried by our 'perfect selves' in frustration at yet another blocked goal. When we do finally express that buried anger we're likely to explode at the most inappropriate moment and before an audience of the most innocent people.

Lisa was happy to have her in-laws stay for Christmas and wanted everything to be perfect for them. Christmas Day went well, but small frustrations and her in-laws' different but perfectly reasonable expectations of the day only increased Lisa's count of her blocked goals. By Boxing Day teatime the changes to Lisa's carefully laid plans, and her tiredness (she insisted on doing everything herself), uncorked her bottled-up frustration like the Christmas champagne, and she exploded. She sobbed that Christmas had been far from the perfect time she'd hoped for and that she was a complete failure. It took her bewildered family a while to convince her that they had enjoyed a wonderful time, spoiled only by Lisa's insistence on working so hard. When the tears were over and everyone had helped clear up, Lisa's mother-in-law playfully suggested that perhaps she should be affectionately nicknamed 'Martha' (see Luke 10:38–42).

The nickname has stuck and reminds Lisa to check her need for domestic and hostess perfection.

GUILT

Perfectionists who carry their early childhood or parental expectations into adulthood may also carry a burden of guilt when they are unable to keep life at a level of 'perfect'. Their inability to achieve or behave as they feel they should can prompt feelings of guilt and shame at not being good enough or worthy enough, often leading to depression, addiction and self-harm. Guilty perfectionists can be very hard on themselves – and on others whom they feel should help to maintain the myth of perfection.

Miranda sought counselling as she watched a family pattern repeat itself. Her domineering mother had been dead for some years, yet she could still 'hear' her voice pushing Miranda to keep the house spotless, just as her equally domineering grandmother's voice had pushed her mother – eventually into mental illness. As Miranda heard herself using the same nagging phrases, threats and guilt-inducing tirades towards her own daughters and their natural teenage untidiness, she was reminded of her own early unhappiness and resulting perfectionism. She made the decision to do something about it before her own daughters suffered.

Perfectionism can affect our emotions at varying levels, from brief flashes of impatience, easily checked, to serious mental illness, but if perfectionism is harming (or threatens to harm) our relationships, we need to seek professional help.

PERFECTIONISM AND OUR SPIRITUALITY

Earlier we mentioned that God loves us unconditionally; that He knows that we are works in progress and that He sees our hearts. His goal for us is anything that will bring us into relationship with Him – for eternity.

Our levels of self-worth, security and significance can be drained by perfectionism. Spiritual drought sets in when we aim for solely human goals. Frustration, anger, anxiety, low moods, low self-esteem and guilt all distract us from being the person God intends us to be.

God has created us to find our sense of self-worth, security and significance in Him. We are designed that way. The Shorter Westminster Catechism says that 'The chief end of man is to worship God and enjoy him forever.' In effect, God says, 'Don't make perfection the goal. Make *me* the goal.' He asks us to live for relationship with Him, growing ever closer. What more perfect goal could there be?

As our relationship with God deepens, we won't do things to be blessed or to be a good Christian or for God to accept us, but just because we love to do things for God! Loosing the ties of perfectionism means that we have fully recognised His grace and unconditional love. He'll be delighted if we do things for Him, and do them well, but that isn't what He wants most. His longing is that we will respond to his love just by loving Him in return.

When we hear those little words 'should', 'ought' and 'must', we have to remind ourselves that from God's point of view the pressure is off; we are free just to love and be loved.

Daphne has been a member in Wendy's church for almost fifty years, but it was nearly forty years before she really understood what it was to have a relationship with Jesus – or even that He wanted her to. Daphne had grown up with an image of God as a tyrannical father, much like her own. She saw Jesus and the Holy Spirit as the alternative versions of God, both designed to check what she was up to. She felt that she could only be as perfect as possible so as not to displease Him: just the way she had placated her father. It was during a Sunday morning sermon on 'God is Love' that the Holy Spirit moved mightily in Daphne's heart. Suddenly she saw that God loved her and that Jesus wanted a close and loving relationship with her. She says that she went to Him that day and sat in His lap like a little child and sobbed with relief. Ever since, Daphne has been like a giggly schoolgirl wrapped up in the arms of Jesus. She was seventy-four years old when she recognised that God doesn't want perfectionism – He wants our love and relationship.

Perfectionism can be rooted in pride. 'If I do a job well it will give me the feel-good factor'; 'If someone sees the value in me, then I feel worthwhile.' Prideful perfectionism can drive us to lust after impressive careers or enhanced status. Of course, there's nothing wrong with having professional or personal goals or desires, but the closer we move to God, the more we will share His desire for us – relationship, from which everything else springs – rather than yearn for human perfection.

Perfectionism pushes God off-centre because it demands something less than our truest self. Galatians 3 says in verse 3: 'Are you so foolish? After beginning with the Spirit, are you now trying to attain your goal by human effort?' And in verse 5: 'Does God give you his Spirit and work miracles among you because you observe the law, or because you believe what you heard?'

Perfectionism also distorts our understanding of the internal and external rewards God gives freely through mercy and grace. A distorted understanding of internal rewards may tell us, 'Of course I am a good Christian; I get everything right' or 'I must be perfect in order to be a good Christian'. This is to misunderstand God's gift of grace – or unmerited favour. His grace and forgiveness do not depend on our being a 'good' person or always getting everything 'right'. We do not have to tick boxes about our faith in order to earn His love. He gives His love and favour and mercy freely. When we acknowledge that fact wholeheartedly, we have an internal reward we can both cherish and live by.

A distorted understanding of external rewards suggests that, 'I will earn myself a place in heaven by doing good things. I will serve on ten church committees, volunteer for everything and make sure I am always the last one to leave the church on Sunday, having polished the pews end to end.' Attending church, praying or reading the Bible and offering service to one another are important aspects of being in relationship with God and with other members of our church family. But they can be little more than signs of perfectionist behaviour: rituals for their own sake which are designed to cover up feelings of guilt 'for being such a bad Christian'.

Amos tells us that God hates false religion, for whatever reason (Amos 5:21–23); that worship is emptied by our indifference to injustice and poverty. Isaiah tells us that God asks another kind of fasting of us – concern for the hungry, the poor and the oppressed (Isa. 58:6–10). We may need to ask whether our perfectionist selves are able to understand and apply the nature of true religion.

Perfectionists might also use Scripture as a sticking plaster solution or a quick fix theological answer, rather than acknowledge and work through a problem, fearing that the outcome might not be perfect.

Emma was worried about her engagement and whether her boyfriend really loved her. Was her decision to marry him the right one? Whenever she worried she told herself that 'in all things God works for the good of those who love him' (Rom. 8:28). While Emma was right to claim that promise, she was applying sticking plaster pastoral theology to a situation that needed to be worked through in more depth. She was also avoiding taking responsibility for her own relationships, not wanting to acknowledge the possibility that her boyfriend might not truly love her in case her perfect view of their relationship was threatened. Yet talking about the issues involved – however imperfect – would have given Emma a firmer foundation on which to build the relationship ... or the wisdom to see that she needed to move away from it.

Peter, as a workaholic and perfectionist, struggled with depression for many years and, when feeling low, would remember a verse his vicar had suggested: 'I can do everything through him who gives me strength' (Phil. 4:13). But he didn't *feel* strengthened and eventually came to believe that this verse wasn't for him. Perhaps he had failed God? His inability to see any truth in the verse when applied to his situation led him to distrust Scripture and to lose hope in God, deepening his depression. What Peter needed was someone who would accompany him on his spiritual and emotional journey; someone who would help him unpack the source of his depression and so bring him out into the light of God's love and faithfulness.

As church families, we often do ourselves a disservice in the area of perfectionism. We expect our church leaders to be supermen and superwomen instead of normal human beings with weaknesses and failings, and then wonder why so many of them fall or fail so easily without our support and reasonable expectation. Our relationship with other church members is similar. We have a tendency to think that the person next to us must pray longer, read the whole Bible monthly, or be more spiritual than us. So we strive to be as good as them – while they are probably thinking exactly the same about us!

Church isn't the place for comparison and competition where perfection is concerned. It's the place to be happily imperfect while being loved and accepted *anyway*.

ACTIVITY

Perhaps you have reached a place where you recognise, and want to work through, a difficult area of your own life in relation to perfectionism. Or maybe you have just discovered that you are more of a perfectionist than you thought!

Choose one object around you – at home or in your workplace – which you feel represents your perfectionism. This may be a mirror strategically placed to check your appearance, a bottle of correction fluid, or a pristine duster neatly folded. Place it where you will see it often, not to induce guilt, but to help you mindfully place that element of your perfectionism in God's hands on a regular basis throughout the day.

REFLECTION

- Take some time to review, and reflect upon, your choices for the activity. Perhaps make some notes on a sheet of paper. Do this silently in the company of our loving and gracious God.
- Don't allow yourself to brood, accuse, lay blame or indulge in cries of 'if only'. Simply bring the things you have written before Him, phrase by phrase, and leave them with Him.

• Read the following prayer and afterwards safely dispose of your notes.

PRAYER

Gracious and forgiving Father God, my words, and tears, are precious to You. You knew these words before they were written. You see my heart and feel my pain. You have watched me all the days of my life and You know why I struggle to be perfect. But You also tell me that I am loved and accepted by You exactly as I am, that I do not have to strive to be better, strain to be first or push myself to limits I can't reach. You simply ask me to walk with You. As I begin the work ahead, stay close to me. Be a place of refuge and encouragement as You remind me that I am already a wonderful, perfect work in progress, in Your Son.

Amen.

NOTES

1. Arnold Lobel, *Frog and Toad Together* (London: Mammoth, 1973) p.5.
2. Judith S. Beck, *Cognitive Therapy: Basics and Beyond* (New York: The Guilford Press, 1996) p.166.

CHAPTER 3

GETTING TO WORK ON PERFECTIONISM

We've defined perfectionism, explored what causes it and considered how it shows itself. So now we need to get to work on achieving the right balance of perfectionism in our lives.

Some of us may choose to recognise the advantages and disadvantages of occasional perfectionist behaviour and work to maintain a helpful balance that works well for us. Others will recognise in themselves – or those they care for or support – a balance of perfectionism that is unhealthy and damaging. Their work may be harder. It may include finding ways to release the perfectionist from the ever-decreasing circle (or the spinning hamster wheel) that is the search for perfection.

WORKING TO UNDERSTAND PERFECTIONISM: RECOGNISING THE BALANCE

Aiming for perfection in our daily lives is not a 'bad thing': insisting on perfection is. It's not that we cross a line from 'good' perfectionism to 'bad', but that we shift further along a continuum, from behaviour that is helpful and healthy, to behaviour that is unhelpful and neurotic. As we've said, our aim is to find balance.

THE PERFECTIONISM CONTINUUM

DISADVANTAGES
Neurotic

ADVANTAGES
Healthy

When perfectionism is associated with active coping and goes hand in hand with natural optimism it can be a helpful strategy with which to cope with the daily ups and downs of our lives. If we can maintain a healthy optimism – and a sense of humour – then perfectionism can work well for us. It keeps us performing at an optimum level, doing our best for God, other people and ourselves, and helps us to live every area of life to the full. It's when we begin to slide in the opposite direction along the continuum, when 'things *must* be perfect', that perfectionism begins to hold us back. Far from encouraging us to do our best, it can make us hesitant, fearful and neurotic.

THE BASIS FOR 'BALANCED' PERFECTIONISM

Our childhood experience will have set early foundations for finding our place on that continuum. Early years' psychologists tell us that for a child to feel loved and valued in order to develop healthy self-esteem, they must have their emotional needs met. Just as we have physical thirsts, we also have emotional thirsts: a thirst to feel secure in our family, to know that we belong, that we matter, that we are safe. Our emotional 'tanks' need to be maintained at a regular level in order to avoid excessive emotional thirst.

To fill those tanks, a child needs to know and experience regular levels of

- security
- self-worth, and
- significance

each of which grows from a foundation of unconditional love offered by parents or carers.

How these tanks were filled in our own early childhood impacts our attitude to perfectionism. If our parents or carers never showed approval, or only showed approval that was conditional ('Mummy will love you if you're a good girl'), if they set ever-higher standards which we found impossible to reach ('Do even better next time!'), our emotional levels will not rise. If those levels remained low as we reached adulthood, it's possible that we will carry on trying to raise them by striving to be perfect in a continuing effort to meet our parents' or carers' expectations. We cannot press an automatic button to top up our sense of security, self-worth and significance, so we choose to move towards a goal that will give us a sense of achieving perfection and gaining the approval, security, self-worth and significance that will 'push the button' for us.

The goal for those of us who are perfectionists is to be accepted, because we believe that acceptance will protect us from failure and insecurity. When we are accepted, we are not rejected; we have not 'failed'. Other people think we are OK, and we move towards our goal.

However, both theory and expectation break down in practice. We might start a new job and, on the first day, decide that we must do this or that task perfectly in order to be accepted. Subconsciously, we tell ourselves, 'I should do this perfectly because I want to be accepted, and when I do it perfectly I will feel more secure in myself, have more self-worth and be far more significant amongst my colleagues.'

But of course, for the perfectionists amongst us, perfection is an elusive thing. We find that however hard we try, in our own view, we never achieve perfection. So, as far as we are concerned, we won't *ever* do things perfectly enough to be accepted. The goal remains unreachable. The day inevitably comes when we survey what we believe to be the wreckage and say, 'I am never good enough.' And our security, self-worth and significance levels drop. It doesn't matter how much our colleagues, partners or friends tell us that we have done a brilliant job, our own perfectionism blinds us to the practical and realistic truth that, yes, a good enough – even the best ever – job was done.

The goal of perfection can become a roller coaster, a precarious ride through life where again and again our security is threatened. We live according to the silent mantra that says, 'I am secure when I reach that goal – perfection – but when I don't reach it I feel insecure and anxious; therefore, I must always be perfect.' Many perfectionists demonstrate a high level of anxiety because they are not meeting their (often humanly unachievable) goals.

Some perfectionists become frustrated and angry with others when *they* don't get things right. Transferring their expectations of self they say, 'You *ought* to do this well.' The fact that the other person hasn't performed as they'd hoped displeases and frustrates the perfectionist as their own goal is blocked. The process is bound to continue in a series of ever-decreasing circles, resulting in damaged relationships.

> Olivia grew up with a mother for whom nothing was ever good enough, almost to the point of abuse. Her father left the family while she and her two brothers were still very young, and Olivia left home as soon as she was able. Whilst she found healing in some areas of her life, even as an adult she found it difficult to release herself from perfectionism. While involved in creative projects with others, she often alienated them by being over-critical, too exacting in her demands, while failing to delegate, or accept the professional expertise and judgment of her peers. Relationship after relationship foundered as she insisted on levels of performance from others that were totally unreasonable. Olivia is now aware of the root cause of her problem, but it will take some time for her to forgive, overcome and heal the damage inflicted by a perfectionist mother in her childhood.

Before working on overcoming areas of neurotic or unhealthy perfectionism we need to recognise the roots of our problem and find a skilled helper or counsellor to work with. This work may involve 'pattern matching' – recognising the voice of a parent, teacher or significant other person in our lives whose message, spoken or otherwise, we still adhere to. We will need to acknowledge, address and process any feelings of sadness, loss or anger which those relationships created in us. This may involve us in the difficult task of seeking resolution, or offering forgiveness – sometimes to those who are no longer alive. Once we choose to find a measure of acceptance of our past, and of our own personal internal make-up, we can find a way forward, step by step.

It's easy to see how much of a handicap neurotic perfectionism can be, whether or not those concerned recognise their behaviour for what it is.

As we look at achieving balance in perfectionism, it is helpful to first identify ways in which a search for perfection can have both a negative *and* a positive effect on our daily lives.

BALANCING PERFECTIONISM IN DAILY LIFE
In the workplace
The disadvantages
Those displaying unhealthy perfectionism will be those who
- unwittingly set themselves up to fail
- set unrealistic deadlines for self and others
- spend too much time on detail
- pay too much attention to areas that require only a cursory glance.

Jack constantly showed his anxiety within the office setting. He was always looking for approval for every piece of work. Yet he infuriated colleagues by what they considered to be wasting time on things that didn't matter to the overall success of a project, or which could be left for the 'tweaking' stage. Jack consequently picked up their disapproval as related to his failure to achieve.

The advantages
Those displaying healthy perfectionism will be those who are
- appreciated at work because they are so good at the fine detail

- highly motivated and very conscientious
- reliable and trustworthy.

> Emily was a valued member of her very creative team. Her ability both to spot potential problems and dot the 'i's and cross the 't's meant that the rest of her team were able to look at the bigger picture while trusting her to mind the small detail. She was always well prepared for meetings and aware of what needed to be done to turn the big ideas into successful outcomes. Emily gained great satisfaction from being able to watch those big ideas develop, while offering her safety net.

In the home
The disadvantages
Those displaying unhealthy perfectionism will be those who
- often cause tension among family members
- live according to the internal pressures of having everything done 'their way', believing it to be the best way
- are overly fussy about neatness, routines, timings.

> Moira refused to allow her children to do anything around the home as they grew up as they would never do it 'properly'. They longed to be able to cook but Moira would get a headache just thinking about the mess they would create. As teenagers they stopped bringing friends home because Moira would watch their every move in case they 'messed things up', leaving all concerned unable to relax. Consequently, Moira had a very tidy, but frequently empty, home.

The advantages
Those displaying healthy perfectionism will
- help create an organised, calm home where busy schedules run smoothly
- be reliable and dependable, keeping appointments, paying bills and maintaining family records
- provide security and consistency for children
- encourage a sense of peace and order that can be internalised.

Now in adulthood, Lizzie speaks fondly of Pam, the mother of her best friend, June. Lizzie's own home life was chaotic. Her mother, an artist, loved Lizzie dearly, but filled the house with friends and parties and was frequently absent in order either to work or to spend time with a number of boyfriends. Pam and June's home, by contrast, was always peaceful, calm and full of the smell of home-baking. Gradually, Pam willingly became a second mum to Lizzie, keeping an eye on her dental appointments and school schedule, to everyone's approval and delight. Lizzie values the contribution of both women in her life, but notes the security and order that Pam gave her at a difficult time as hugely influential.

Relationships
The disadvantages
Those displaying unhealthy perfectionism will
- apply their high standards to others, becoming critical and demanding
- react defensively to anything that borders on criticism
- be prickly and hard to live with in close relationships
- possibly avoid letting others see their mistakes, resulting in tense behaviour.

Newly-weds Jeff and Louise attended relationship counselling as both were concerned about Louise's behaviour. Jeff was finding her increasingly difficult to live with; she picked at his DIY efforts around the house, shouted at him if he tried to help her do anything she considered to be 'her job', and often found it hard to relax. The tense atmosphere that resulted was making the early days of their marriage difficult and they wanted to 'nip things in the bud'. Over many weeks of counselling, Louise and Jeff were helped to understand that Louise had taken her perfectionist expectations of relationships into marriage. They were gently helped to find ways forward, and Jeff counted it a real achievement when he finished hanging a pan rack in the kitchen (not exactly perfectly straight) to Louise's applause.

The advantages
Those displaying healthy perfectionism will
- express confidence in a partner, friend or colleague's ability
- sensitively maintain their relationships and keep in touch with friends and family
- remember birthdays, anniversaries and 'important' days
- resist impulsively jumping into relationships where they may be hurt
- not take offence easily
- take time to listen, celebrate others' achievements and perceive their needs.

Lola was overjoyed when friends in her post-natal group anonymously entered her for a 'Best Friend Ever' competition – and she won! The women concerned said that despite learning to cope with her own new baby, she had been a constant source of support and encouragement for all of them. She always listened to problems and gave time to help others, while maintaining her own personal boundaries and the needs of her baby and husband. She remembered to ring friends when she knew they may be having a bad day, and encouraged her husband to round up all the other new dads for a curry and a beer to celebrate surviving six months of fatherhood!

Ourselves
The disadvantages
Those displaying unhealthy perfectionism will
- suffer a good deal of internal angst over 'getting it right'
- lose sleep over today's – or tomorrow's – potential failures and successes
- often rehearse and relive incidents, conversations and events in real agony when trying to meet high expectations
- regret or become cross at their own prickliness or hurt in the face of what they see as rejection or criticism.

Melanie was loved and respected in her church, not just as a friend, but as a gifted speaker and pastoral team member. But she often felt low, insignificant, and as if she would never be accepted. Her church friends were puzzled and sometimes hurt by her prickliness. Despite constantly being told how much she had to offer and how greatly she was appreciated, Melanie lived in a continual state of worry, often spending sleepless nights replaying conversations and situations in which she felt she could have done better.

The advantages
Those displaying healthy perfectionism will
- gain a good deal of satisfaction from a job well done
- set healthy and realistic goals for tasks, and feel pleased when

they are met, even if no one else notices
- take a healthy pride and self-respect in their appearance, their home and their work, and praise others with genuine delight
- give themselves an equal balance of challenges and rewards, effort and relaxation.

Imogen looks forward to Christmas every year, not just because of the celebrations, but because she loves the few days after Christmas when she sets herself the task of putting her flat straight for the New Year. While still in festive mood she turns out cupboards, cleans and polishes, sorts out clothes and papers and generally gets things in order – often with a leftover mince pie and a sherry in tow! Sometimes she invites friends who are lonely, involving them light-heartedly in her chaos and taking the opportunity to make them feel special. She says that it is a tradition which gives her great satisfaction.

Healthy perfectionism in our daily lives is about finding balance rather than making constant comparison. It's about working and hoping for the best, not straining and struggling for it.

But if we do recognise ourselves (or others) in some of the scenarios above, what might we do? How might we tackle, and reduce, the negative impact that perfectionism has on our lives?

WORKING TO OVERCOME PERFECTIONISM: RESTORING THE BALANCE

For those of us who have edged towards, rushed headlong into, or found ourselves unwillingly gripped by the pull of perfectionism, there may be some hard work to do. Perfectionism is a difficult habit to break. It is often etched into our very DNA and will stay imprinted even as we try to erase it.

However sincere we are in wanting to change our perfectionist behaviour, or however much we want to help someone else to do this, we – and they – can come up against almost immovable blocks which may need longer, deeper work with a skilled therapist.

HINDERING BLOCKS TO OVERCOMING PERFECTIONISM

Understanding how we often shy away from, and protect ourselves from, the pain of change can help us to address unbalanced perfectionism, thus bringing acceptance and the beginnings of healthy change.

1. 'I am unable or unwilling to consider alternative ways of thinking.'
   This may be because:
   a) Our belief is so strong that we believe our thoughts are balanced and true.
   b) We have come across information that contradicts our belief, so we ignore it.
   c) We have difficulty in admitting a mistake.

2. 'My perfectionism is not causing any significant problem.'
   This may be because:
   a) The benefits of perfectionism may seem to outweigh the costs.
   b) Perhaps we are not aware that our high standards cause problems for ourselves and/or others.

3. 'I don't believe I can change.'
   This may be because:
   a) I believe this is who I am (it is part of my personality).

4. 'It's not the right time to address my perfectionism.'
   This may be because:
   a) Life is too full and hectic with too many demands so now
      may not be the best time to start working on perfectionism.
      (On the other hand, if life is exhausting with it, always busy
      and stressful, now may be as good a time as any.)

5. 'I am too anxious to face the change.'
   This may be because:
   a) I fear making mistakes, and fear failure, ie I fear not being
      perfect even in shaking off unbalanced perfectionism.

To reach the point of being able to begin to overcome unhealthy
perfectionism, it is helpful to work in three areas:

1. ACCEPTANCE

The first step to changing perfectionist behaviour is acceptance.

Recognising that certain behaviours impact our lives negatively,
having a sincere desire to change, and understanding both the
costs and the benefits of change are an important prerequisite to
working towards a successful outcome that can be permanently
maintained.

We may need to recognise the roots of our behaviour and
to understand whether we are 'pattern matching' (ie following
a pattern of perfectionist thought we have always followed, for
instance the internal voice of a parent or teacher).

Maria found it helpful to use a Dictaphone to record the negative messages she was still hearing from parent and teacher, as and when they popped into her head during the week. These were then 'played back' in her therapy sessions so that her therapist could help her formulate responses to challenge – and eventually render powerless – what she was hearing. Alongside this, she meditated on scriptures of God's love and unconditional acceptance of her. At the end of her sessions the tapes were destroyed, with great glee.

In his book *Too Nice for Your Own Good*,[1] Duke Robinson writes about the importance of 'accepting our acceptance', a phrase he attributes to Harvard theologian, Paul Tillich. He explains that because 'we've already been accepted by the love that defines what it means to be human', it is important that 'we accept our acceptance and live in the freedom love lavishes on us'. Unfortunately, many of us have experienced conditional acceptance as a way of life, and with this comes the message that we are not valued just as the person we are; hence, the importance of accepting the reality of the truth that God accepts us and affirms us as people of infinite worth and value.

2. FACING FEELINGS

Secondly, we need to face up to and process any feelings that arise – sadness, anger or frustration – by:

- Uncovering feelings: 'This is how my feeling is manifested – through behaviour/self-talk/what others close to me report.'
- Identifying feelings: 'That's a feeling of guilt/shame/regret/ striving.'
- Accepting feelings: 'I can see and acknowledge that I am

showing this feeling in this behaviour.'
- Giving the feelings some meaning: 'I can understand why I might feel this way.'

When we are able to accept our own internal make-up – our personal history and experience – we can acknowledge the contribution, both positive and negative, each has made to who we are. Our perfectionist behaviour can be identified as part of that make-up, but also as something that can be changed.

If we are seeking to help those struggling with perfectionist behaviour, we must be wise companions on their journey, encouraging emotional honesty and offering acceptance in a non-judgmental way.

> Sophie was shocked but relieved to recognise that much of her seemingly habitual anger, highlighted by her perfectionism, could be traced back to her mother's high expectations of her. She had achieved so much academically, but felt that nothing was ever good enough for her mother. Sophie was only able to get help once her mother had died, when she found support and a safe place to release her suppressed anger and hurt.

3. ACKNOWLEDGEMENT
Thirdly, we need to acknowledge the costs and benefits of changing perfectionist behaviour :

> 'But I've always done it like this. What will happen when I don't?'
> 'Others may think I am incompetent or lazy.'
> 'The level of performance of others around me may decrease.'

'I'll lose control of stuff!'

But

'I will have more time to enjoy myself.'
'I will be easier to live with, criticising my family less.'
'I would be less concerned about what others may think of me.'
'I won't be so stressed.'

Perfectionists need skills and tools which can help them through the anxiety that causes their perfectionism: tools which will help them identify the likely negative and positive results of changing their behaviour. This could take some time.

We often cling to perfectionism when we want to avoid the anxiety change brings. Consequently, a cycle of perfectionism is maintained or even widened.

Change must occur in

- our thoughts
- our beliefs
- our behaviour
- our spiritual life

Change in these areas will inevitably impact both our emotions and our spirituality.

CHANGING PERFECTIONIST THOUGHTS

There are three ways in which we can help ourselves – or encourage others – to change ways of thinking.

Before we can change a thought we need first to identify it, challenge it, and then look for a different perspective on our situation before replacing it with an alternative thought.

IDENTIFICATION

It's not easy to identify our own perfectionist thoughts – from our viewpoint, they are entirely appropriate. It might help us to gain some objectivity if we were to imagine a barrister questioning us before a judge:

'Are these thoughts really appropriate, or are they biased?'
'What beliefs are they based upon?'
'Have they always been there and, if so, are they reliable, or have they become distorted?'

We may need outside help – an advocate if you like – to support us as we identify our own thought patterns and examine them rigorously. Long-held habits can be hard to break.

CHALLENGE

Once a thought is identified and questioned as to its origin and honesty, we must challenge it. Challenging just one recurring perfectionist thought can begin to break the mould. For example:

Thought: 'This house should be perfectly tidy before I go out. I ought to vacuum.'
Challenge: 'Why? Is that a timescale demand? Who needs to see it "perfectly tidy"? If it's basically clean and organised, why does it need to be "perfectly tidy"? Who says? Me? Why?'

The 'shoulds', 'oughts' and 'musts' we use are clear indicators of the kinds of demands we make upon ourselves as perfectionists. Who says I 'should'? Where is it written that I 'ought' to? Why 'must' I? Whose internal rule or script is that? Who says I have to follow it?

In essence, we look for evidence to challenge the perfectionist thought. Our challenge can include any ammunition we might find: logic, science, pragmatic suggestions, experience, and the opinion of friends. As we fling the ammunition towards the 'shoulds', 'oughts' and 'musts', we begin to ask ourselves: 'What effect does this perfectionist thinking have on what I do?'; 'Is this healthy for my long-term goals ... and am I really getting any closer to them by behaving this way?'

FINDING A DIFFERENT PERSPECTIVE

Then we look for a new and different perspective. Even if we don't agree with that perspective at first, or can't define it precisely with words, it's still helpful to hear this new view, just as if we were at an organised debate respectfully listening to all opinions. We might discover that we agree and change our own opinions in the light of this newly presented evidence!

Let's go back to the need for a 'perfectly tidy' house for a moment. A good and trusted friend might say, 'Come on, let's go. It's tidier than mine will ever be!' or 'The fluff will be back tomorrow anyway!' Or perhaps they'll highlight the benefits: 'We'll have time for a cappuccino in that lovely coffee shop if we go now. You need a break.'

If there's no (earthly) friend available, we could imagine what God might say. How does He see the situation? Would He prefer me to spend time with a friend, or time with the vacuum cleaner? Does

He want me to be a Mary or a Martha today (Luke 10:38–42)?

Wendy has a small print of a painting by Vermeer hanging on her kitchen wall. It shows Mary sitting at Jesus' feet and Martha leaning over His shoulder with a serving basket in her hands. It's clear what Jesus is saying: 'Leave it for a while, Martha. Come and sit with Mary and Me.' The kitchen seems to Wendy to be a good place to be reminded that everything doesn't have to be perfect, and that time with friends and time with God are more important than a spotless kitchen floor and a complicated meal. She knows she has never regretted putting the call of friends or God before housework, but she has often regretted putting housework before God and friends. That little picture reminds Wendy of a lesson she is sometimes slow to learn in her (albeit occasional) quest to make things 'just right'.

CHOOSING AN ALTERNATIVE THOUGHT

Once we have found a different perspective, we can form an alternative thought that takes into account all the gathered evidence and a broader vista. It may take some time to feel comfortable with that changed view. We all know that changed habits take a while to become truly ours. For a time they can be more like wild rabbits than new habits – jumping around in and out of our minds! But the more familiar we become with them, the more we can tame them and make them our own.

When we look back at those unvacuumed but perfectly OK carpets, our new thought might be: 'Friends and coffee first, fluff later!' or 'Well, it's amazing how clean that carpet still looks. It can rest easy until tomorrow.'

Jane has invited friends and neighbours around for an informal barbecue as she does every so often, but as they start to arrive she realises that she has run out of meat. Jane becomes embarrassed, anxious and frustrated with herself. Thoughts buzz around her head as she tries to think of a solution: 'I ought to have bought more! I should have noticed we'd finished those frozen sausages and chops. I ought to have known that all my neighbours would turn up.' As Jane stands in her larder surveying the empty freezer, she begins to challenge and replace her perfectionist thoughts: 'Well, how lovely that so many people have turned up. They must love being with me! They must love my cooking, too. Who says I should have done better? I did my best with the knowledge I had. My friends and neighbours know me well – they're unlikely to judge me just because I'm short of a sausage or two. They'll know it's because I'm always cooking for them! There's plenty of salad and bread left, there's plenty of drink, and everyone seems to be enjoying themselves, in spite of running out of meat. I can always put out an appeal for any spare meat in other people's freezers. People love being asked, and it'll bring even more unity and a bit of fun to the event.' Jane closes the freezer, turns on her heel and yells from the kitchen window: 'Anyone got any beef burgers in their freezer?'

CHANGING PERFECTIONIST BELIEFS

Core beliefs can be deeply held and are often hard to change. Sometimes, to change perfectionist beliefs we have to ask, 'Who am I trying to please?'; 'Why do I drive myself in this way?'; 'What is my motivation?'; 'Is it the real me or habitual attitudes from the past?'

David, in challenging his core belief: 'I'm worthless', was prompted to answer the question, 'Who says I am worthless?' Chris helped him to answer in a positive way and more fully than he'd hoped. She said, 'Imagine that you are driving down the motorway and are involved in a crash. You are buried under the wreckage. An ambulance, the police, firefighters and even a helicopter arrive on the scene and spend hours carefully lifting you from beneath your shattered car. If you're worthless, why do they do that? They don't even know you! But as a person, your life is worth an infinite amount. So they will work long and hard to save you.' David realised the truth of what Chris had suggested. If those who didn't even know him would do so much, how much more must he be worth to family and friends – and, wonderfully, to God?

Chris has used this illustration with many clients. Tears flow as people begin to realise for the first time that they are a person of worth because they are a unique, precious human being, rather than a machine of perfectionism.

God says – and we can say to others – that we each have infinite value, whatever our underlying beliefs may suggest to us. None of us is perfect, but each of us has great worth. We are made in His image.

CHANGING PERFECTIONIST BEHAVIOUR
One effective way of changing perfectionist beliefs is to change the behaviour they lead to, as such behaviour maintains the attitudes and predictions of perfectionism.

Exposure-based strategies – where a feared object or situation is confronted – bring perfectionist beliefs out of hiding. The fear is then shown up for what it is, becomes recognisable and is consequently less of a threat.

Exposure-based strategies

An excellent way to test the validity and accuracy of perfectionist thoughts and predictions is to carry out small experiments, a process known as hypothesis testing.

One client of Chris's, a perfectionist, felt he could never really ask for anything – help, advice or directions – because he believed that he should always know the right answer: such a request would be seen as a weakness. Chris encouraged him to be bold. They agreed together that he would go into the supermarket and ask for something crazy that he knew wouldn't be stocked (a green plastic frog, perhaps, or a jar of blue gooseberries) in order to test his hypothesis – his hypothesis being, 'If I ask for something, especially something that's unavailable, people will laugh at me and that would be awful because it would mean I am not perfect, but weak.'

So, very bravely, he went into the supermarket and asked the assistant for his outlandish item. A few minutes later, he came out of the shop beaming, and reported to Chris that the assistant had been very helpful and not at all dismissive: 'Yes, it was fine. She didn't laugh at me, and I feel so much better.' Then he said, 'I can't wait to tackle the next thing on our list.'

When we want to change our perfectionist behaviour we will experience a certain amount of anxiety before 'exposure'. But the more we face small, achievable goals, the more progress we will make.

There is nothing wrong with having high standards, but sometimes we need to challenge them. 'I can't stand being late. I must be on time!' is a common refrain. But when it is sincerely meant and causes problems to the extent that we arrive earlier and earlier or experience greater stress in order to be on time, our behaviour, and our belief, may require challenge. Why can't I 'stand being late'? What will happen if I am? These questions are asked by challenging the behaviour that accompanies the belief. We could give ourselves permission to be just a few minutes late. This is not so as to cause inconvenience to anyone else, but in order to understand that the worst does not usually happen because we are just one or two minutes late.

The belief that 'I cannot handle an untidy house, it has to be tidy!' often produces behaviours classed as OCD (obsessive-compulsive disorder) behaviours. Changing behaviour in order to change beliefs could begin with just leaving a door ajar or a chair rearranged for a few days, before moving on to leaving one room untidy. As we discover that the world does not end as a result of an open door or a chair that isn't perfectly angled at ninety degrees – or when the benefits of abandoning a particular behaviour are recognised – our behaviour will gradually change.

Similarly, recognising that 'I spend hours choosing what clothes to wear' may be a common cry amongst women, but it may also flag up a perfectionist attitude to appearance which means that we need to set time limits for choosing clothes and dressing.

Adjusting standards
Much of our behaviour is dictated by expectations and standards which are often inherited from others. These standards can be unrealistic, impractical and not 'us' at all, but we get trapped in them. Sometimes it is perfectly acceptable, even important, to lower standards in order to have more achievable goals.

We could ask ourselves these questions:

- Are my standards reasonable, given my circumstances and resources (time, energy, money) and abilities?
- Are my standards giving me a healthy outcome?
- For whom does my standard have to be good enough?

Answering these questions will help us to set our own standards and decide what our priorities are.

Adjusting goals
It's not enough to want to 'become less of a perfectionist'. The only way to evaluate whether our behaviour is becoming less and less influenced by our perfectionism is to set small achievable goals which are realistic and specific. These are goals which are both short-term – the changes we want to make over the next few days and weeks – and long-term – the changes we want to make over the next year, or longer.

For instance, the goal

- 'I will not be so critical of my husband'

might be made more specific and achievable as

- 'I will not criticise my husband for not putting his shoes away'.

The more specific the goal, the easier it will be to come up with long-term, gradual strategies that, when threaded together, facilitate lasting change in behaviour.

For example:

General goal	*Specific goal*
Become less perfectionist with appearance.	Be able to go out for a social evening after spending no more than an hour getting ready.
Become more tolerant of my children.	Allow my children to make a mess, provided they clear up by the end of each day.
Be less concerned about what others think of the work produced in my office section or team.	Delegate my everyday letter-writing to my very capable secretary.

Overcoming procrastination

The phrase 'Never put off until tomorrow what you can do today' is easily changed to 'Why do today what you can put off until tomorrow?', especially by those of us who are great procrastinators. But, as we discussed earlier, procrastination, far from being a sign of laziness, low standards or non-commitment to goals, can be a sign of perfectionism.

We have already recognised that people procrastinate for a variety of reasons:

- fearing they won't be able to do a job well
- not knowing where to start
- fear of letting others (or themselves) down.

Felicity knew that she must begin her dissertation. Her research was gathered and her key outcomes were written, but the actual act of sitting down to write up her research was becoming a huge burden: she was simply unable to start. Whenever she sat at her keyboard she would think of a million other things that needed doing. Finally, through sharing her writing paralysis with her tutor, Felicity was helped to understand that her reluctance to work wasn't laziness, but a fear of failing. Felicity had done well on her course; her dissertation was the final piece of work which would help determine her degree result. She genuinely feared that she would do so badly that it would sink her chances. Rather than completing her work only to discover her failure, she had been reluctant to begin at all.

We can work through procrastination by using a simple strategy to enable us to take a step-by-step approach to any task we face reluctantly.

If we are able to break the job or project down into small, manageable tasks that are achievable in short bursts of time, we can then feel a sense of achievement along the way, and reward ourselves with a cup of tea or a walk, instead of feeling overwhelmed by the larger picture.

Changing thoughts, beliefs and behaviour all contribute to overcoming perfectionism. But for those of us who live a life of faith, our spiritual journey is at the heart of the matter.

Our final chapter offers practical suggestions to equip us on our spiritual journey to wholeness.

ACTIVITY
Think of a recent situation or event in which you know

your perfectionist thoughts took control, perhaps leading to perfectionist behaviour. Apply what you have learned in this chapter to those circumstances:

Situation _____

Emotions experienced _____

Perfectionist thoughts _____

Challenging the thoughts _____

Different perspective _____

Alternative thoughts _____

What can you learn from this to take forward into another similar situation?

Write yourself a motto or catchphrase (like 'friends now, fluff later!') as a reminder.

REFLECTION

'Character is that which can do without success.'
(Ralph Waldo Emerson)

- Do you agree with that statement?
- Would God agree with it?
- What will you *do* as a result?

PRAYER

Lord God, as I work through these issues of perfectionism, often taking three steps forward only to take four back, remind me that I *am* making progress. Reassure me that You do not look at my 'improvement rate' or ask for a 360 degree review. Neither do You look at my 'To Do' list – but at my heart. Lord, help me find balance in perfectionism. Amen.

NOTE

1. Duke Robinson, *Too Nice for Your Own Good: How to Stop Making Nine Self Sabotaging Mistakes* (New York, Boston: Warner Books, 2000).

CHAPTER FOUR

BEYOND PERFECTIONISM: SPIRITUALITY

Earlier, we reminded ourselves that the pressure is off; that by God's grace, through His love, we are free to be who we are in Him – we don't have to be perfect. That doesn't mean that we don't aim high or try our best, but that in Christ our best is good enough for God. If our best is good enough for God, we need to come to a place where it is good enough for us. Acknowledging that fact wholeheartedly – and living believing it – can bring true freedom from perfectionism.

Some of us will follow a pathway as we come to acknowledge and understand what that freedom truly means – a pathway that passes through

- brokenness
- repentance

- abandonment, and finally arrives at
- freedom

BROKENNESS

The first step to freedom is the understanding and experience of brokenness and humility before God, acknowledging that we can't reach perfection of any kind alone; however much we try and strive and struggle, we *can't* be perfect!

The systems and structures that we (and the world) put in place in the pursuit of perfection are not of God, but of humankind. They are our determined efforts to push God to one side and place our own agenda at centre stage. But once we cast off those systems and structures, which demand so much of us, we can see ourselves as we really are – not through critical eyes, judged by the world's standards or with our own expectations, but as God sees us: made in His image but very, *very* human. Brokenness reveals our humanity to us and replaces God at the centre of our lives. And when we recognise our humanity, and its limitations, we recognise God in a new way.

Chris had a real sense of her humanity when her daughter was ill:

It was a difficult time that brought so much to the surface. I hated the muck I found within myself. But God, in His love, brought me to a place of brokenness. It wasn't fun seeing just what sort of person I am! But I realised that so much of overcoming perfectionism lies in identifying that we have so much of ourselves inside, driving us. We say 'I want to get there in order to please me. I want to get there so that no one rejects me' rather than 'Lord, my relationship with You is the most important thing. Fill me up with Yourself and show me that when I walk with You, we'll get there together'.

When we come face to face with our humanity we begin to understand how little we can do alone. In knowing God we come to realise that He enables us to do more than we ever believed or imagined, in *His* strength.

Wendy, when she worked for a large national charity, was often asked to speak at events. She hated it. Absolutely terrified, she would pace car parks and hotel rooms beforehand, desperate to give a perfect performance. Often she was 'OK', sometimes even 'quite good', but she always *felt* that she was absolutely dreadful. After one event, recognising that she was relying on her own strength and gifts, she prayed that God would not allow her to speak at any more events unless it was in *His* strength and with *His* gifting. It was several years before she was asked to speak again and, remembering the prayer and bringing the situation before God, she then began a journey in which she increasingly learned (and is still learning!) to rely on and have confidence in Him, even at a lectern. As a result, God has developed a special gift of communication from that broken place – 'I can do everything through him who gives me strength' (Phil. 4:13).

So, God calls us to a partnership. It is 'God and me doing it together', rather than 'Me striving to get it right alone'! That partnership sometimes involves us in a process that may be uncomfortable but which leads to a strengthening of relationship and a clear moving forward:

- Suffering: a perfectionist often suffers with the consequences of their thoughts and behaviour. Into this place the partnership of God brings comfort.
- Despair: never meeting the impossible goal leads to desperation and loss of hope. Into this place God brings joy – and hope.

- Felt unworthiness. Like Job (Job 40:4) we feel unworthy. In this place of unworthiness God touches us with His love.
- Death to self: an acknowledgement that God wants to be central, and a willingness to welcome Him. This leads to new life in Jesus.

In this place of close communion, God calls us to put to death the determination to find a way to make this life work by creating sure-fire systems, together with the belief that such a way exists. Instead, brokenness reveals to us just how unlike Jesus we are, but also bids us come to Him, allowing Him to mend our brokenness so that we can live – and live in *His* strength and gifting.

Morwenna had pushed herself to achieve at work after her husband left her with two children to care for and largely support. She felt this responsibility keenly and was determined that they should be able to maintain the lifestyle they had always known. But long hours working and trying to deal with all her responsibilities at home made Morwenna feel as if she was increasingly running on empty. Her daughter became difficult, suffering from both her dad's and her mum's absence, and the crunch came when she was suspended from school for abusive behaviour towards a teacher. Morwenna felt that she had failed herself, the children and God; she felt unworthy; unloved and desperate. With the help of the pastoral director at her church, Morwenna came to a place of surrender to God. She recognised that she could not make progress without Him, or build the personal resources she needed to care for her daughter and son. Eventually, Morwenna simplified her life by moving to a smaller house and arranging to work part-time. Her children were old enough to recognise that compromise had to be made in lifestyle, but also that their mum had made decisions that would enable them to be together more and to rebuild their lives as a family – God's way.

Inevitably, brokenness will involve finding ourselves in a place of:

REPENTANCE

Living God's way involves choices.

Firstly, we *choose* to decide that always trying to be perfect is unhealthy; it can only be a dead-end street. We begin to understand that living essentially to please others is a fruitless journey, but that living to please God is an adventure.

That choice involves repentance – a turning round, choosing to think differently (not just saying sorry) and moving away from the old way of thinking and behaving into God's way of living. We do so ultimately because we love Him and want to please Him, not because we 'must'.

Secondly, we *choose* to stop making unhealthy choices which push us to the wrong side of the perfectionism continuum. This might sound simplistic: 'If only it were that easy!' we cry. But until we actually commit ourselves to stop doing something, setting specific goals and step-by-step objectives, we remain stuck in thought and belief and behaviour.

Steven got into the habit of drinking after work with his colleagues in order to keep up with the 'in' crowd, and to keep in touch with what was happening in the business. What started as a pint before the train home gradually turned into longer and longer drinking sessions. Although Steven was growing in favour with his boss and workmates, he knew that he was not living God's way. He realised things had gone too far when one evening, after several hours of drinking, he found himself in a lap-dancing club. Fearful of being thought 'odd' or 'prissy', Steven had gone along with the crowd, but sat in the club feeling horrified with himself and the path he was taking in order to succeed at work. On the way home in the nearly empty train, Steven confessed his miserable state to God and asked for forgiveness. He asked God to find a way forward which would enable him to live the right way. A few weeks later, Steven was offered another job out of the blue, for less money but closer to home, and with a company whose ethics and director he admired and respected. Steven felt God had honoured his repentance and the commitment he had made to change.

Brokenness and repentance will in turn lead to:

ABANDONMENT

Abandonment is an act of letting go – and letting go of ourselves. As such it involves us in risk. We don't know what it will lead to, but we know we want to be released from what went before. Abandonment to God, however, does not involve anxiety about what might come next. We can trust God to hold us and do the best for us, as our letting go is a letting go in faith.

We will never be able to abandon ourselves to God as long as we think we can change without Him. When we earnestly long to live to please God and to be more like Jesus, we will abandon ourselves to His Spirit. We recognise that 'I can't do this in my own strength, Lord God, I need more of You'. In other words, we surrender.

So often when we think of surrender we think of weakness, and defeat. But that isn't the kind of surrender that God calls us to as we work against perfectionism. Surrender to God is a beautiful surrender: a giving up of self so that so much more than self can be given back by God in return. When artists surrender paint and creativity to paper, they produce something beautiful. When musicians surrender music to their instrument, they produce a beautiful sound. When writers surrender words to the page, they communicate with passion.

If we avoid surrender, we miss out on the unique 'self' God designed us to fulfil. It is only by finding our true selves in God, and leaving ourselves in His hands, that we are free to be who we really are. Anything that leaves self at the centre, unsurrendered to God, pushes God out and leaves us, ultimately, unfulfilled.

A surrendered self doesn't mean that we are forced to become someone else; a lesser version of who we are, or someone more serious, sensible or straight-laced. Rather, abandonment leaves us free – free for God to make something beautiful out of the unique self He created in us. It allows Him to work with His original pattern to bring about what He intended for our lives. We are enabled to become the person He planned: the Designer version, if you like!

A life lived in surrender to the Designer is ongoing, reflecting our value as a work in progress. It is not an alternative and instant route to perfection.

Sophie describes herself as an 'elastic' Christian! She says that she is always pinging back and forth from God's way to her own. Sometimes she can trust Him and walks ahead without hesitation; at other times, she grabs back the 'elastic reins that control her life' and stretches them in what she believes is a better direction. Again and again, she says, she finds herself pulled back onto the right path 'on the slack', with God's love. Once she gets there – back in the right place with God – it would be easy for her to get angry with herself for having gone her own way yet again. Instead, she abandons herself to God knowing that He is just pleased to see her back in the right place, and that both of them hope she will stay there this time! But for now, the important thing is that her focus is a loving, forgiving and welcoming God. She recognises that true abandonment to Him is not a one-off, but a continual adjustment of her 'elastic' according to His ways.

Surrender *will* be a lifelong process. There are times when we surrender a little of ourselves, and times when we surrender a lot. We'll even have times when we take back part of what we have surrendered. God knows that the journey of surrender is a difficult one. Jesus took the ultimate journey of surrender; He knows of our struggles.

But the journey of surrender is also a creative one. God often does His most creative work in the dark times; think of Jesus on the cross in full surrender. But He also knows – as did His Son – the joy that waits for us at the only truly perfect end: an eternity of perfection with God.

So, the only way to live for today, and be made perfect in eternity, is to

- Abandon ourselves to a God who loves us so much that He values us more highly than we will ever understand.
- Abandon ourselves to a God who created us, and knows our weaknesses as well as our strengths.
- Rely utterly on God's sovereign grace to bless as He chooses and when He chooses, rather than striving to earn God's blessings by being perfect.

FREEDOM

What we are working towards is a freedom that will save us from lapsing back into perfectionism by liberating us to express the best of ourselves and serve our deepest interests.

God gives us a new freedom to be who we are; a freedom in which it is OK to be perfect and OK not to be. A freedom whereby we can strive and work for excellence, but take it easy on ourselves when we feel we fall short; a freedom to glance upwards at God's estimate of what we are doing and catch His smile, rather than berate ourselves for having failed yet again.

The old self said, 'My will be done.' The new self is saying, 'Your will be done.' The old self said, 'I expect good things to happen.' The new self says, 'I am on the journey to becoming like You, Jesus.' The old self said, 'I am in control.' But the new self says, 'I have surrendered my life. God is now in control.' The old self said, 'I live to be blessed.' The new one says, 'I live to know and love Christ.' That way is freedom. This freedom will enable us to choose

When to try to be perfect and when not to
When making a special celebration cake for a friend or relative, we will try to make things perfect, for their delight (knowing that even if the decoration comes out all wrong they'll still love it). But when we're asked up onto the stage to join in with the orchestra at a fundraising event, but don't read a word of music, we'll happily bang the triangle with a great big grin on our faces!

When to strive for excellence and when to take it easy
When the report we're writing will make the difference between getting the funding we need to build the new children's centre

or not, we'll give ourselves time to research, and listen to broad opinion. Then we'll write a bid that is as near perfect as we can make it. But once that bid is submitted, we'll accept that there is only so much funding to go round, pray about the outcome and know that we have done our best.

When to do what we need to do, even when others won't like it
When we're asked to cut corners, be creative in our accounting or do things 'the way it's always done' rather than the right or ethical way, we'll check our motivation, explain our criteria and do the job to the best of our ability God's way – whatever the response of other human beings.

As perfectionists, it could be easy to believe (or we have been brought up to believe) that a life lived God's way must be a life lived perfectly – even a life lived narrowly; a life with little opportunity and even less delight, ruled by regulations and warnings and Bible verses that shriek into our lives out of context and with little care. But far from being a life lived according to more do's than don'ts, life God's way is a life of true freedom leading to safe – if often daring – choices, all encircled by His love. When we live a life with God, we exchange a dull and dragging march accompanied by an out of tune military band for a glorious dance in riotous colour to the most joyful of music. Life God's way gives us freedom of a shape and design we can never imagine.

But that freedom is something we need to nurture and protect as we go forward. At times we will begin to know a stirring of the Holy Spirit deep in our being; a new identity; a new inclination; a new power. At other times we will know frustration, wondering if we have taken a wrong turn, lapsing back into perfectionism for security. In *both* places we can find Jesus, put our hand into His and go on along the pathway He has designed for us. Transformation takes time and effort and a close walk with the One who longs to transform us – and we *will* make progress. However faltering that progress at times, we *are* being transformed into the likeness of Jesus. We are beautiful works in progress.

TRUE CONFIDENCE

True confidence is about letting go of ourselves in our search for perfection, and finding our confidence in God; relying less on ourselves and increasingly relying on God's strength. Not just leaning on Him in the tough times, but being filled with His strength and belief in us at the best of times. Jeremiah tells us 'But blessed is the man who trusts in the LORD, whose confidence is in him' (Jer. 17:7). So how do we find confidence in Him?

Firstly, we find confidence in the Father[1] as He tells us what He believes about us. God tells us that we are loved, and He tells us over and over again. In fact, confidence in God's love directly provides what we need: security, self-worth and significance. We are *secure* so that whatever happens to us, we are safe in God's protection. Jesus says, 'I give them eternal life, and they shall never perish; no-one can snatch them out of my hand' (John 10:28). We are *worth* so much that Jesus gave His life for us, and for the whole world (John 3:16). We are *significant* in that we are made in God's image (Gen. 1:26).

God's love is constant, solid and unchangeable. It holds us firm, safe and close. In that relationship we have a perfect foundation upon which to build a confident future, free from the relentless struggle for perfection. For, as Paul says, 'If God is for us, who can be against us?' (Rom. 8:31).

Secondly, we can have confidence in the Person of Jesus, God's Son, as our role model. Too often we choose role models whom we think are perfect, just as we want to be. But the only really perfect role model is Jesus. As we watch the way He lived and worked, we can identify hallmarks and characteristics that we can bring into our own lives.

Jesus came as a servant (notice that He was a *servant*, not a doormat!) anointed by God. Everything He did pointed to His Father and unfolded the kingdom He'd come to share. His priorities were people and prayer: the people He served, taught and had compassion upon; the people He engaged in long conversations; the people who became His friends. People mattered to Jesus.

How might our attitude to life be transformed if we made our priorities those of people and prayer? Taking our eyes off ourselves and fixing them on God and others, in service, will also take our eyes off our own agenda and move God back to centre stage.

Thirdly, we can find confidence in the Person of the Holy Spirit as our guide, comforter, inspiration and source of other-worldly power. When we invite the Holy Spirit to be part of all we are doing we can relax in the knowledge and understanding that God is with us. Our goals can be shaped His way, not ours. Often we find we slow down, take time to reflect and stop fretting and struggling. A task or job may still need to be completed but we have a helper, comforter and guide within, throughout and beyond our own efforts. More than that, the Holy Spirit empowers us, gifting and leading us in ways we can hardly believe. When our life is lived in surrender to God, it is lived in surrender to the Holy Spirit and all of His resources.

When our confidence is rooted in the love of God the Father, modelled on Jesus and inspired by the companionship of the Holy Spirit we are able to share God's love wholeheartedly with others and 'be Jesus to them'.

When the woman at the well met with Jesus in the Gospel of John (4:4–42), she was searching for something to remedy her emotional and spiritual emptiness. She had gone the wrong way and made the wrong choices, trying hard to fill her own life with what she thought was love. Yet she failed in relationships and never made the grade either in her own eyes or those of her community. Then Jesus met her. He offered her love and life. She accepted, and could not help but run off to share His offer with others – even the very people who had rejected her. She also found worth, confidence and a secure future through meeting the only man who would ever really love and accept her – whatever she had done.

RESTING IN GOD'S LOVE THROUGH RELATIONSHIP

The woman at the well teaches us that love begins with acceptance and grows in relationship. God tells us that He is with us always, but He also asks that we be with Him in the context of a loving relationship.

Wendy's husband works in London during the week, while she stays at home in Devon. It's not yet the right time to move in order to be together, but it's an odd existence. Although Wendy and her husband know that they are thinking of each other through the week and speak on the telephone, there would be something wrong if their love didn't mean they looked forward to Fridays, for that's when they know they can be together.

When we love someone and know they love us, we want to be with them, and they want to be with us. God is no different. He longs for us to be with Him. He doesn't have to try to fit us into His schedule, or complain when we want another five minutes of His time: He longs for a relationship that is real and honest and practical.

The relationship we have with God goes far beyond any earthly relationship. The more we open ourselves to Him, the more His love melts away the things in us that really stop us moving forward and changing positively. Love is the dominant, primal energy of life. It brought us into being and, if we allow it, it will carry us through life. We become whole to the degree that we are able and willing to receive and give love. Love offers us unconditional acceptance, withholding judgment even when it *is* deserved. Receiving God's love can liberate us from the never-ending struggle of trying to be perfect. As we journey away from perfectionism we can begin to look at life through the lens of love and see acceptance and intrinsic worth rather than punitive judgment and rejection. It is never too late to know, feel and live in the accepting, enveloping warmth of God's love.

So how do we find a way forward from perfectionism through a day-by-day life with God?

In practical terms we might commit ourselves – in the love of God, not under pressure! – to the following:

1. *A daily surrender to God as we wake*
This is a time when we acknowledge God's love for us. This may be as simple as a one-line prayer: 'Thank You, Father God, that You love me so much. Help me take Your love into this day.' Or we could use a favourite prayer, song or reading that reminds us that God loves us, that we are a work in progress and that whatever we do today in His name and for Him is good enough

for Him – indeed, it will delight Him! (We might also like to choose to surrender to God again at the end of the day, before we sleep.)

2. *Finding time to soak in and reflect on the Word of God, the Bible*
Determine to do this not as a study exercise or in pursuit of the 'right' answers, but simply letting the word of God 'dwell in [us] richly' (see Col. 3:16). Richard Foster[2] says that God tells us often that He is with us and, through the Bible, asks us, 'Will you be with Me?' Foster offers a wonderful model for this kind of reading of the Bible – *lectio divina* – where we understand God's Word with heart as well as mind, letting the love of God enfold us as we read, lifting our faces to His. So often we read the Bible for what we can get out of it, rather than what God wants to give us through it.

3. *Taking a fresh look at prayer*
So often prayer becomes a competition with ourselves, or even with others. We 'must' pray for thirty minutes/get up at 5am/ go to every prayer meeting/use the right words. But when we are able to understand prayer as part of an intimate relationship with God, an extended conversation, our prayer will be transformed. It doesn't even need words; often, we can just enjoy God's company in silence. Isn't the ability to do that the sign of any close relationship? Surely God must prefer that to a rushed 'To Do' list of my needs and requests for guidance! Yes, of course we are told to bring our needs, fears and anxieties to Him in prayer, but to do so in the context of relationship.

4. *Finding a mentor/spiritual director*
As we move forward on our journey away from the search for

perfection, it may be helpful to share and pray with a wise and listening friend, faith mentor or spiritual director; someone to whom we can be accountable, in an atmosphere of grace, love and gentleness, for the progress we are making.

5. *Giving ourselves to true service*
If our lives are modelled on the life of Jesus, they will be lives of service. Not lives that are dominated by the needs and demands of others, but lives in which we find time and space to serve those who need our care and attention – perhaps especially those who are unable to give in return – and doing so within clear and healthy personal boundaries. There is nothing like fixing our eyes on God – and concentrating on meeting the needs of others – to make us forget our own concerns, stresses and inadequacies.

6. *Knowing that worship ... is life!*
Everything we do is worship. If we were able to live as if each act, conversation, observation and appreciation were worship, how our lives would be transformed! For most of us, it will be enough to find a few moments scattered throughout our day to turn our hearts and minds to God with gratitude, in awe, in joyful delight. But as one of Wendy's church elders reminds the church family: 'Clearing away and straightening chairs can be the highest form of worship.' Perhaps we can convert some of our perfectionist traits into an element of worship. (Go straighten those chairs!)

7. *Taking time to find, and know, joy*
We are so often so busy with things that need to be done that we let our busyness push the joy out of our days. Choosing to laugh, to have fun, to enjoy the simple things in life – a beautiful piece

of music; a coffee with good friends; kicking the leaves – is an important part of gaining a right perspective on life. Taking just one minute to watch a spider weave its web, to contemplate the sunset, to generally be aware of our surroundings, is time well spent. The minute can seem like an age at first, but consider how often we 'waste' a minute waiting for the kettle to boil, a train to arrive or the microwave to 'beep'! A minute (or more) for joy is never wasted.

As we invite God to be a closer companion on our journey from perfectionism – and if we keep step with Him – we will begin to know acceptance, love and a sense of fulfilled promises. God wants the very best for us and will help us to know *His* best, rather than ours. Remember what the apostle Paul said: 'If God is for us, who can be against us?' (Rom. 8:31).

ACTIVITY

Buy yourself a spiral-bound notebook in which you can begin a journal. Don't feel that you 'should', 'ought' or 'must' write in it every day. That would just be another too perfect expectation! Instead, begin to write down some of the things you might do – perhaps chosen from the suggestions above – to surrender your life to God in more practical and intimate ways; ways which will help you to focus less on the expectations and demands you make of yourself, and more on God's desire for relationship. Go back to it as and when you want to. Record something you have prayed, or something you feel God may be saying to you on your journey from perfectionism to Life … and watch the story continue to unfold.

REFLECTION

- Take a minute, as suggested above, to enjoy the joy!
- Think about how you feel that God wants relationship with you, daily life with you and that He wants this more than anything you could do or achieve for Him.
- Record a written commitment to spend time with God in the midst of your moments of joy next time you kick leaves, play a piece of music you love, appreciate a view or enjoy the happy gurgle of a baby.

PRAYER

Gracious and loving Father, I am overwhelmed that You accept me as I am, that You love me just the same and that You long for close relationship with me. Help me to be with You because I *want* to be, not because I feel I 'ought to' or I 'should'. Help me search for Your heart and find in it a place of peace and assurance. Thank You that You so love this work in progress that is me. Amen.

NOTES
1. These ideas are developed in and adapted from Wendy Bray, *True Confidence* (Farnham: CWR, 2008).
2. Richard Foster, *Life with God* (Grand Rapids, MI: Zondervan, 2008).

AFTERWORD

TEN RULES FOR A STRESS-FREE LIFE

Thou shalt not be perfect, nor even try to be.

Thou shalt not try to be all things to all people.

Thou shalt leave undone things that ought to be done.

Thou shalt not spread thyself too thin.

Thou shalt learn to say 'no'.

Thou shalt schedule time for thyself and thy supportive network.

Thou shalt switch off and do nothing regularly.

Thou shalt be boring, untidy, inelegant and unattractive at times.

Thou shalt not even feel guilty.

Especially thou shalt not be thine own worst enemy but be thy best friend.

Author unknown

National Distributors

Day and Residential Courses
Counselling Training
Leadership Development
Biblical Study Courses
Regional Seminars
Ministry to Women
Daily Devotionals
Books and Videos
Conference Centre

Trusted all Over the World

CWR HAS GAINED A WORLDWIDE reputation as a centre of excellence for Bible-based training and resources. From our headquarters at Waverley Abbey House, Farnham, England, we have been serving God's people for over 40 years with a vision to help apply God's Word to everyday life and relationships. The daily devotional *Every Day with Jesus* is read by nearly a million readers an issue in more than 150 countries, and our unique courses in biblical studies and pastoral care are respected all over the world. Waverley Abbey House provides a conference centre in a tranquil setting.

For free brochures on our seminars and courses, conference facilities, or a catalogue of CWR resources, please contact us at the following address:
CWR, Waverley Abbey House, Waverley Lane, Farnham, Surrey GU9 8EP, UK

Telephone: **+44 (0)1252 784700**
Email: **mail@cwr.org.uk**
Website: **www.cwr.org.uk**

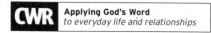

CWR Applying God's Word
to everyday life and relationships

More insights from our wealth of experience

The Waverley Abbey Insight Series brings together biblical understanding and practical advice to offer clear insight, teaching and help on a range of issues.

Insight into Addiction – Find out how addictions take hold and how their power can be destroyed at the roots, never to rise again.
ISBN: 978-1-85345-505-6 **£7.99**

Insight into Anger – Learn how to diagnose the deep roots of inappropriate anger and discover how to overcome resentment, rage and bitterness.
ISBN: 978-1-85345-437-0 **£7.99**

Insight into Anxiety – Discover just what anxiety is, who is at risk of it and how to help those who suffer from it.
ISBN: 978-1-85345-436-3 **£7.99**

Insight into Forgiveness – Find freedom from the past through the power to forgive, and see how living a life of forgiveness brings release and freedom.
ISBN: 978-1-85345-491-2 **£7.99**

Insight into Bereavement – Find out what emotions arise when a loved one dies, we experience divorce or the loss of a job etc, and learn how to work through the grieving process.
ISBN: 978-1-85345-385-4 **£7.50**

Insight into Eating Disorders – Discover the root causes of eating disorders and deal effectively with the denial and self-destruction that trap most sufferers. Written by a former anorexic and the founder of an eating disorders charity.
ISBN: 978-1-85345-410-3 **£7.50**

Insight into Self-esteem – Cultivate healthy self-esteem by deepening your relationship with God.
ISBN: 978-1-85345-409-7 **£7.50**

Insight into Stress – Recognise stress and its causes, and learn what you can do about it.
ISBN: 978-1-85345-384-7 **£7.50**

Prices correct at time of printing and exclude p&p

Available from CWR by calling **+44 (0)1252 784710**, online at **www.cwrstore.org.uk** – or from your local Christian bookshop.